The MAILBOX®
The Education Center®

Bulletin Boards & Displays

Student-Centered Displays

- Reinforce the curriculum
- Showcase student work
- Help manage classroom routines
- Create a positive learning environment
- Help motivate students

Use throughout the year!

Managing Editor: Hope Spencer

Editorial Team: Becky S. Andrews, Kimberley Bruck, Sharon Murphy, Debra Liverman, Diane Badden, Thad H. McLaurin, Lynn Drolet, Kelly Robertson, Karen A. Brudnak, Jennifer Nunn, Hope Rodgers, Dorothy C. McKinney, Amy Adam, Nancy Alley, Cindy Barber, Mederise M. Burke, Andrea Chestney, Jennifer Cochran, Virginia Conrad, Christine Cooley, Karen Cottingham, Colleen Dabney, Juli Engel, Nicole Evans, Ann E. Fisher, Phylene Fizzuoglio, Susan Foulks, Tracy Grant, Dawn Guidry, Tonya Heartsill, Cynthia Holcomb, Robin Hull, Peggy Hurd, Laura Johnson, Deva Jones, Jennifer L. Kohnke, Patricia Laker, Courtney Limpert, Nancy Menno, Stephanie Moss, Teri Nielsen, Donna Pawloski, Kathy Scavone, Erin Sherry, Joyce Wilson, Stacie Wright

Production Team: Lori Z. Henry, Pam Crane, Rebecca Saunders, Chris Curry, Sarah Foreman, Theresa Lewis Goode, Greg D. Rieves, Eliseo De Jesus Santos II, Barry Slate, Donna K. Teal, Zane Williard, Tazmen Carlisle, Kathy Coop, Marsha Heim, Lynette Dickerson, Mark Rainey, Sheila Krill, Karen Brewer Grossman

www.themailbox.com

Manufactured in the United States
10 9 8 7 6 5 4 3 2 1

Table of Contents

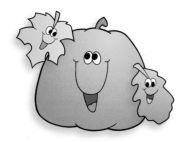

Skills Grid

	Back-to-School	Fall	Winter	Spring	End of the Year	Anytime
Language Arts						
adjectives	11			36		54
alphabetical order		18	30			53
book review			27			57, 58
consonant blends			29			
contractions		13		39		
descriptive writing		16, 18	26, 29, 30	33		57, 64
fact and opinion						60
homonyms	9					
homophones				44		66
letter writing						59
multisyllable words				34		
parts of speech				45	49	
phonics						54
plurals		20				
poetry				46		
reading motivation		19				59
spelling				45		
suffixes						60
synonyms					47	55
verbs			25			
vocabulary		16		34, 39, 43		
vowels		18		34, 43		
word families					48	56
writing	6, 11	14, 19, 20	23	35, 37, 38, 45	49, 50, 51, 52	58, 64
Math						
fractions		16		44		
graphing			27			62
math facts	9		22	39, 41	48	60, 65
measurement			25	34		
multiplication facts		17		35		61, 67
place value						66
plane figures						61, 64
solid figures				36		
telling time						63
temperature			31			
Venn diagram				37		59
vocabulary						65
word problems			26	37		62
Science						
animal facts			28	37		
plant life cycle				38		
Social Studies						
Black History Month			32			
Cinco de Mayo				42		
Columbus Day		14				
Earth Day				40		
fire safety						55
Hanukkah			22			
Kwanzaa			23			
Martin Luther King Jr.			31			

Quick Tips

Change in an Instant!

Label a class supply of top-loading page protector pockets each with a different child's name. Staple the pockets on a bulletin board that displays students' work. Slip a sample of each child's work in his pocket. To change his work sample, simply slip it out and replace it.

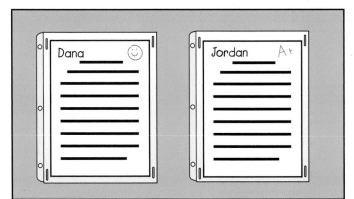

A Personalized Border

Divide the class into groups and give each group a colorful sentence strip. One group member uses a crayon or marker to write her name on the strip. Then she passes the strip to another group member. That child uses a different-colored crayon or marker to write his name. Groups continue in this manner until each child has written her name on a strip. Staple the strips around a board for a colorful, unique border!

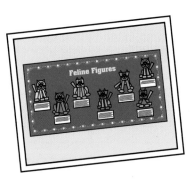

Photo File

Photograph each bulletin board once it's assembled. Store the photos in a file box or photo album under appropriate headings. When it's time to put up new bulletin boards, you'll have ideas at your fingertips.

A Variety of Backgrounds

These reusable materials make fun alternatives to bulletin board paper!

- shower curtains

- fabric

- bedsheets

- plastic tablecloths

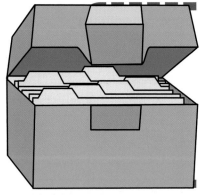

Back-to-School

A Sweet Slice of Summer

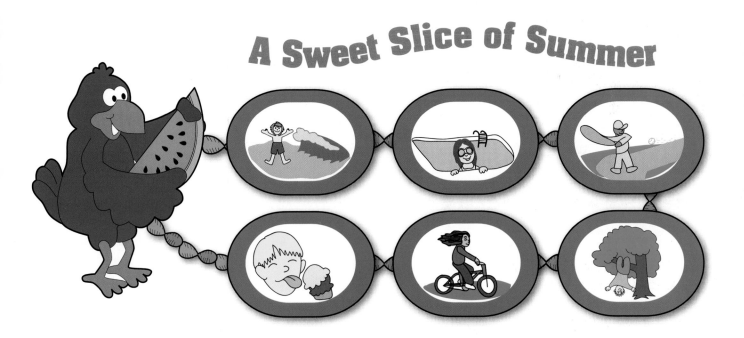

Post a crow cutout (enlarge the pattern on page 74) on a wall beside lengths of twisted green crepe paper vines. Have each child draw a picture of his favorite summer memory on a paper oval. Next, instruct him to glue his oval onto a slightly larger sheet of green paper and then trim the green paper to create a border. Invite each child to share his favorite summer memory; then mount the watermelons on the vines.

Encourage students to set goals for the school year. Post on a board an enlarged copy of the dinosaur pattern on page 75. Have each child write a goal for the upcoming school year on a colorful dumbbell (pattern on page 76) and cut it out. Post the dumbbells on the board.

Give students the opportunity to introduce themselves to their classmates. Have each child draw a self-portrait and write a description of herself on a strawberry (pattern on page 77) and cut it out. Then have her glue her strawberry onto a slightly larger sheet of red paper and trim the paper to create a border. Encourage each child to share her description with the class; then post the berries above a large basket cutout.

Students' good qualities are the focus of this door display. Post an enlarged copy of the tiger pattern from page 78 on a door decorated as shown. Give each child a copy of a fish pattern on page 76 or 79. Have the child list one of her good qualities on her cutout before she colors the pattern and cuts it out. Display the fish on the door.

Post a large orange cutout. Then have each child draw something she hopes will happen this school year on each of three pie-shaped cutouts. Have her glue her shapes to an orange semicircle to make an orange slice. Invite students to explain their illustrations to the class.

Post a large treasure chest cutout. Have each child cut a coin or gem shape from construction paper. Then have him write his name and add details. Display the cutouts inside the treasure chest.

No Bones About It, We're a Great Class!

This cheerful dog welcomes students to school! Post a dog cutout (enlarge the pattern on page 80) and make a class supply of bone halves (patterns on page 79). Have each child personalize a bone half and cut it out. Attach the bone halves to the board as shown.

Use the dog again. See page 55.

 Variations

- **We're Boning Up on Homonyms**
  Have each child cut out two bone halves and write one word in a pair of homonyms on each half. Post the corresponding bone halves together around the dog.

- **Getting Our Paws on Math Facts**
  This interactive board helps students practice their math facts. Program several dog bowl cutouts with different math fact answers and post them on the board. Write different math facts on individual bone half cutouts. To use the board, a child uses Sticky-Tac to attach each bone half to its corresponding bowl.

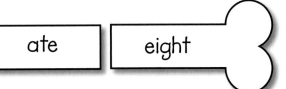

To make this undersea display, ask each child to color and cut out a scuba diver cutout (pattern on page 81). Mount the cutouts on a trimmed piece of blue bulletin board paper. Also give each child a colorful paper fish (patterns on pages 76 and 79) on which to write his name and something he hopes to learn this school year. Display each child's diver and fish together.

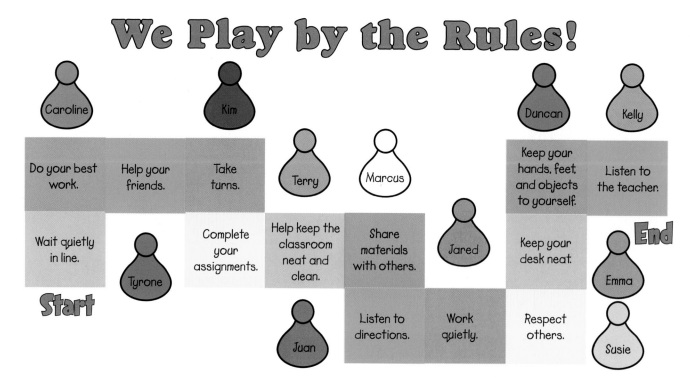

This bulletin board makes an attractive display *and* serves as a reminder of good citizenship! To begin, have each student write on a five-inch construction paper square one way to make the classroom a safe and positive place. Post the projects to make a game trail. Then have each child cut out and personalize a game piece. Add the game pieces to the display.

Jumping for Joy Over a New School Year!

Post a large trampoline cutout on a wall. Invite each child to draw a picture of herself jumping into the air. Have her cut out her drawing and post it above the trampoline.

✔ Student Activities

- **Adjectives:** A student writes on a blank card an adjective describing how he feels about the new school year and attaches it to his likeness. Invite students to use the display for a back-to-school writing assignment.

- **Writing to a prompt:** A child responds to a prompt such as
  —Second grade will be so much fun because…
  —This year I want to learn about…

Excited

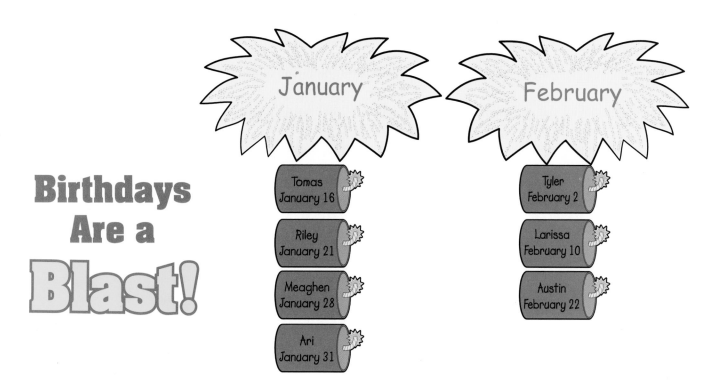

Birthdays Are a Blast!

To prepare this birthday display, use glitter glue to make a firework burst for each month of the year. Then have each child write his name and birthdate on a firecracker cutout (pattern on page 82) and decorate it as desired. Post the completed firecrackers under the corresponding month.

Show students that cooperation keeps the classroom neat and tidy. Label a lily pad cutout for each classroom job and then post the lily pads on a board. Have each child personalize a copy of the frog pattern on page 82 and cut it out. (Laminate the cutouts for durability, if desired.) To assign jobs, post one frog on each lily pad. Store the unused frogs until it is time to rotate jobs.

Fall

Just "Ripe" Contractions

To prepare this interactive display, post a tree cutout within students' reach. Label a desired number of apple cutouts (pattern on page 83) with two words that can be combined to make a contraction. Label the same number of leaf cutouts (pattern on page 83) each with a different contraction that corresponds with an apple. Post the apples on the tree and place the leaf cutouts nearby. To use the display, a child uses Sticky-Tac to attach each leaf to the appropriate apple.

We're Nuts About School!

My favorite thing about school is my teacher because she is nice.
by Cameron

I like learning about animals.
by David

I like reading books at school.
by Addison

Lunch is my favorite part of the school day!
by Carrie

I like when we play outside on the playground.
by Svetlana

My favorite thing at school is singing songs in music class.
by Luis

Art is my favorite thing about school because I like to draw pictures.
by Hope

School is fun. I learn lots of things here.
by Quincy

Encourage students to share their favorite things about school! Post an enlarged copy of the squirrel pattern on page 84 on a board. Have each child write her name and her favorite thing about school on an acorn (pattern on page 85) and cut it out. Post the acorns on the board.

A Wave of New Holidays

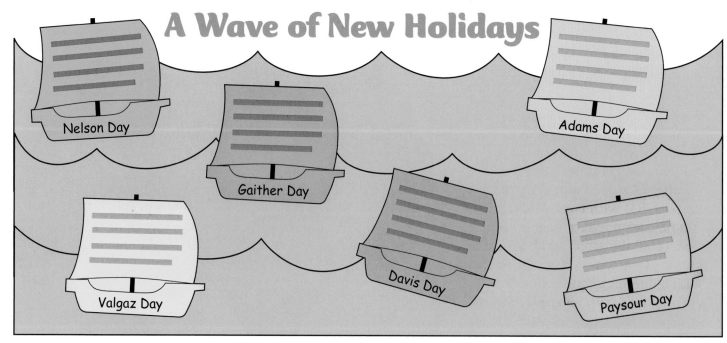

Nelson Day

Gaither Day

Adams Day

Valgaz Day

Davis Day

Paysour Day

After introducing Columbus Day to your students, have each child imagine that there is a special day named after him. Have each student write about his day on a copy of the boat pattern on page 86. Display the boats as shown.

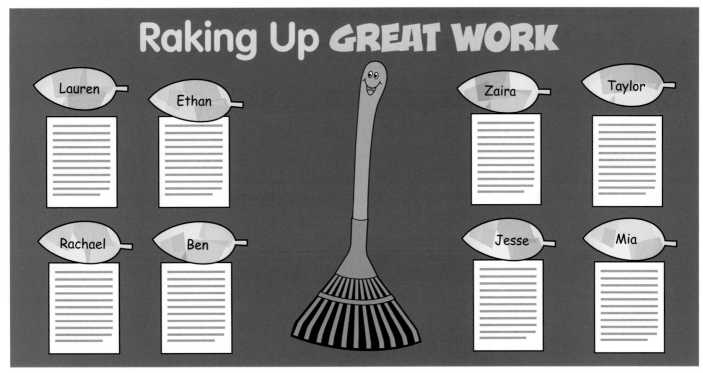

Raking Up GREAT WORK

Enlarge the rake pattern on page 87, color it and cut it out, and post it on a wall. Have each student make a leaf (see below). Post each child's leaf near a sample of his best work.

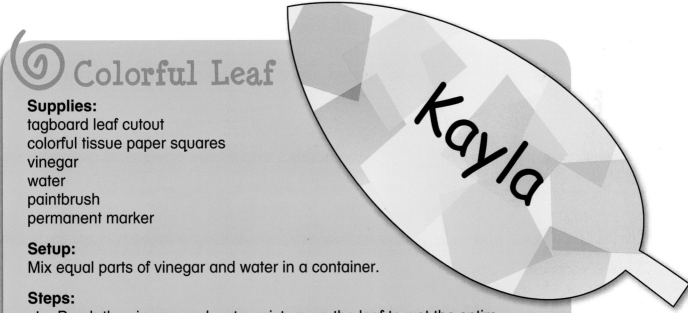

Colorful Leaf

Supplies:
tagboard leaf cutout
colorful tissue paper squares
vinegar
water
paintbrush
permanent marker

Setup:
Mix equal parts of vinegar and water in a container.

Steps:
1. Brush the vinegar and water mixture on the leaf to wet the entire surface.
2. Place a tissue paper square on the leaf and brush over it with the liquid.
3. Continue in this manner until the leaf is covered with tissue paper squares.
4. After the project is completely dry, remove the tissue paper squares and write your name.

This display serves as a handy fraction reference! Have each child make brown thumbprints around an orange construction paper circle so that it resembles a pumpkin pie. Next, have each student draw lines to divide her pie into a designated number of equal slices. Then have her label each slice of her pie with the corresponding fraction. Post the completed pies on a board.

✳ Variations

- **What's Your Favorite Slice?**
  Have each child decorate a construction paper triangle to resemble his favorite type of pie. Then have him write to describe his pie using adjectives to explain what he likes about it. Display each child's writing sample along with his slice of pie.

- **Putting Pies Together**
  Label each slice of a pie shape with a related vocabulary word. Cut the pies apart and give one slice to each student. Lead students in reassembling the pies according to the vocabulary words. After each pie has been properly assembled, post it on a board under a corresponding heading as shown.

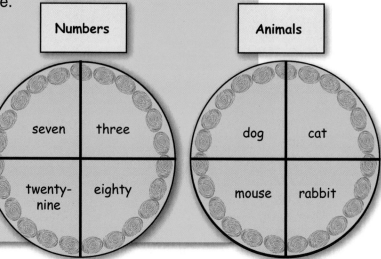

Math Facts Football

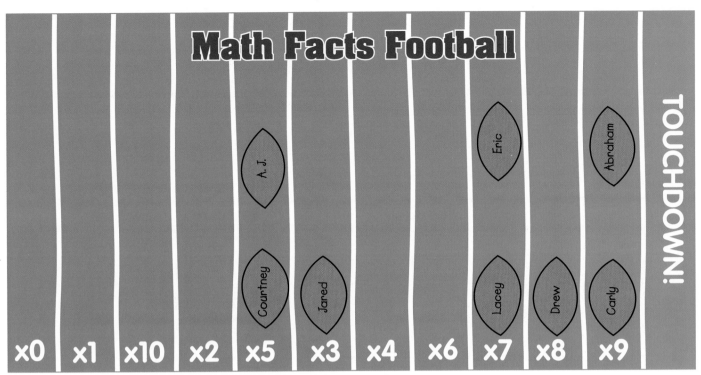

Motivate students to learn their math facts! Draw yard lines on a length of green bulletin board paper, labeling each section with a different multiplication factor and writing "touchdown" in the last section. Invite each child to personalize and cut out a football shape from construction paper. When a child masters the first multiplication factor, have her mount her football in the corresponding section of the field. As she masters additional factors, she moves her football accordingly. After a child has mastered each set of math facts, she scores a touchdown!

Here's a great way to showcase students' work throughout the fall! Post a scarecrow cutout on a board (enlarge the pattern on page 88). Then make a class supply of pumpkin cutouts. Attach a photo of each child to a pumpkin labeled with his name. Display each child's work sample with his pumpkin. Change the work samples as desired.

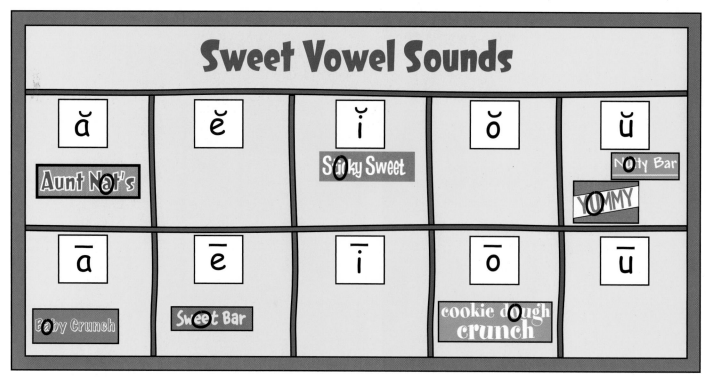

Sweet Vowel Sounds

Have students save their empty candy wrappers from Halloween for this board. To prepare, use yarn to divide a board into ten sections. Label each of ten blank cards with a different short- or long-vowel sound and attach one card to each section of the board. Next, place the candy wrappers in a container near the board. A child chooses a wrapper and reads the name of the candy. After he identifies a vowel sound in the name of the candy, he circles the corresponding vowel with a permanent marker and attaches the wrapper to the appropriate section of the board.

✔ Student Activities

- **Alphabetical order:** A student lists the candy names from the board in alphabetical order.

- **Descriptive writing:** A student creates a new type of candy and writes to describe it.

My candy is called the Chocolaty O'Chip. It is a chocolate bar with potato chips crushed up and mixed into milk chocolate. It is salty and sweet. The potato chips are crunchy when you bite into the bar. It is delicious!

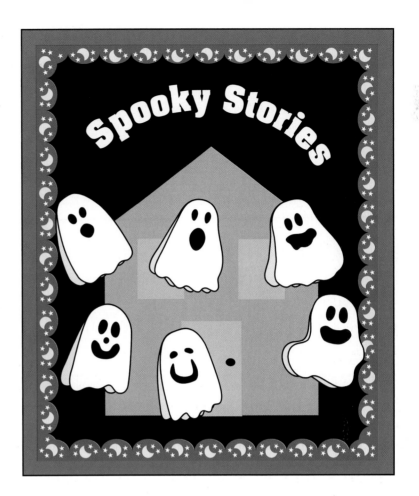

Prepare a haunted house cutout and mount it on a board. Have each student fold a sheet of white paper in half and then cut it to make a ghost-shaped booklet. Have her write a spooky story inside. Then have her add a ghostly face to the outside of her booklet. Display the completed ghosts on and around the haunted house.

Gobbling Up Genres

Make a desired number of enlarged copies of the turkey pattern on page 89. Label each turkey with a different genre and post it on a board. Prepare a supply of feather cutouts and place them in a container near the board. After a child reads a book, invite him to write the title and author of the book on a feather; then have him attach the feather to the matching turkey.

Make a supply of pilgrim and corn cutouts (patterns on page 90). Label each ear of corn with a different singular word. Give each child an ear of corn and a pilgrim cutout. Have him write the corresponding plural on the pilgrim. Then have him color his pilgrim. Mount the pilgrims and corn cutouts on the board.

Student Activities

- **Sentence writing:** A student writes a different sentence for each plural word on the board.

- **Writing to a prompt:** A student responds to a prompt such as
  —The pilgrim grew an enormous ear of corn!
  — My favorite way to eat corn is…
  — If I were a pilgrim, I would…

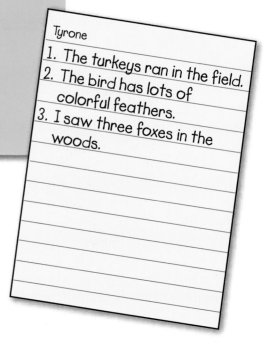

Tyrone
1. The turkeys ran in the field.
2. The bird has lots of colorful feathers.
3. I saw three foxes in the woods.

Winter

Winter "Accomplish-mints"!

Ava helped Marcy on the playground.

Ricky completed all of his assignments.

Jackson walked quietly in line.

Samson was a good friend.

Jenny helped Ms. Engel grade papers.

Amy shared her crayons with Stefan.

Put the spotlight on student behavior with this sweet display. To prepare, post a candy dish cutout and have students decorate a supply of four-inch white circles to make peppermint candies. When a student demonstrates exceptional behavior, write her name and a description of her behavior on a peppermint. Mount the candy above the candy dish.

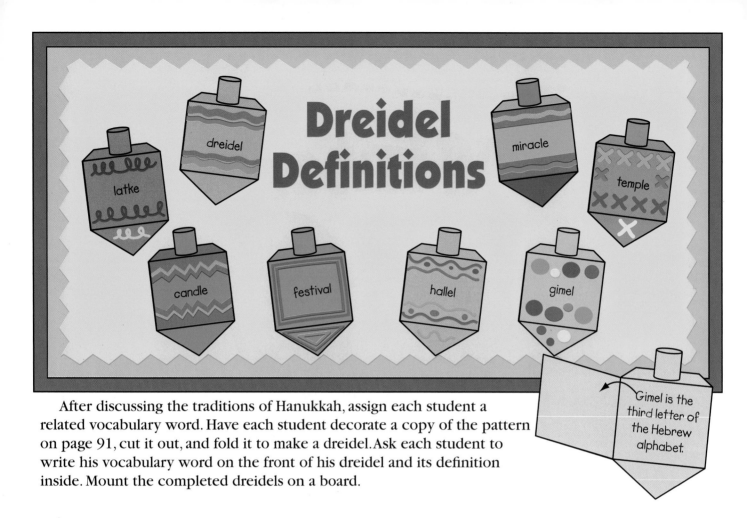

Dreidel Definitions

After discussing the traditions of Hanukkah, assign each student a related vocabulary word. Have each student decorate a copy of the pattern on page 91, cut it out, and fold it to make a dreidel. Ask each student to write his vocabulary word on the front of his dreidel and its definition inside. Mount the completed dreidels on a board.

Gimel is the third letter of the Hebrew alphabet.

Variations

- **Dreidel Math**
  Have each student decorate a copy of the pattern on page 91, cut it out, and fold it to make a dreidel. Then have him write the numbers in a fact family on the outside of the dreidel. Ask him to list the math facts that correspond with the fact family inside.

- **Hanukkah Riddles**
  Invite each child to decorate a copy of the pattern on page 91, cut it out, and fold it to make a dreidel. Then have him write a question about a Hanukkah tradition on the outside of the pattern and write the answer inside.

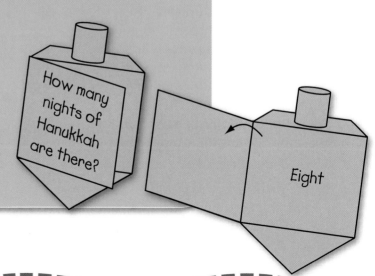

How many nights of Hanukkah are there?

Eight

Giving Literary Gifts

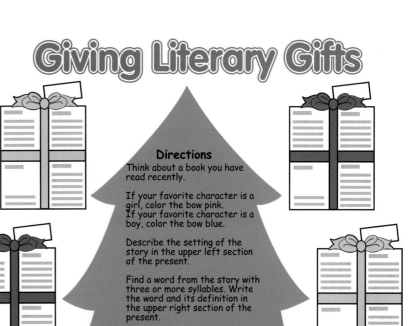

Invite students to respond to a book shared in class or to one they have read independently. Write the directions shown on an evergreen tree cutout and then post it on a wall. Give each child a copy of the gift box pattern on page 92. Have him decorate the gift box according to the directions and then cut it out. To complete the display, mount the gifts around the tree.

Directions

Think about a book you have read recently.

If your favorite character is a girl, color the bow pink. If your favorite character is a boy, color the bow blue.

Describe the setting of the story in the upper left section of the present.

Find a word from the story with three or more syllables. Write the word and its definition in the upper right section of the present.

Draw and label a picture of an important object in the story in the lower left section of the present.

List a character and three words to describe him or her in the lower right section of the present.

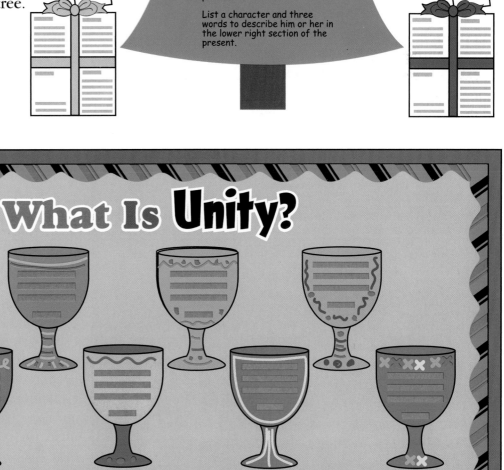

To begin, share with students that one of the seven principles of Kwanzaa is unity and that it is traditionally represented by a unity cup. Give each child a copy of the unity cup pattern on page 93. Have each student write her definition of *unity* on her unity cup. Then have her decorate her cup and cut it out. Display the cups on a board.

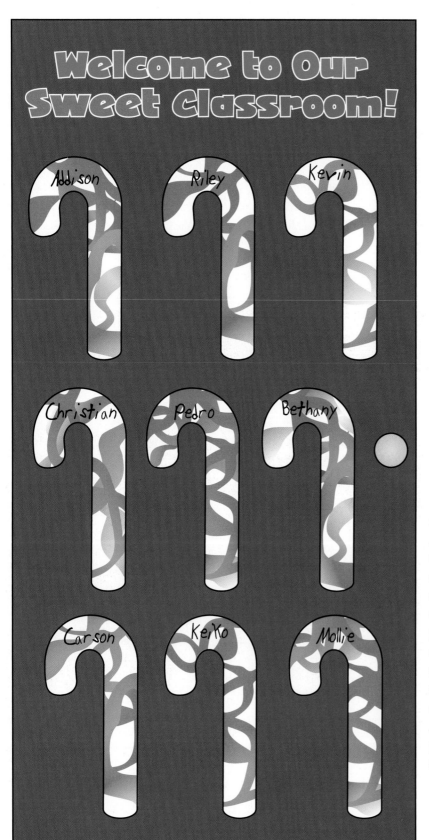

Welcome to Our Sweet Classroom!

Addison

Riley

Kevin

Christian

Pedro

Bethany

Carson

Keiko

Mollie

Welcome visitors to your classroom with the scent of peppermint! Add a few drops of peppermint extract to diluted red tempera paint. Have each child place a copy of the candy cane pattern on page 94 in a shallow container and drop a few drops of the prepared paint in each corner of the container. Drop in a Ping-Pong ball and have the child tilt the container to make the ball roll through the paint and over the candy cane to make stripes. After the paint is dry, have each child personalize his candy cane, cut it out, and attach it to the classroom door.

Wonderful Winter Wear

27 inches

17 inches

15 inches

23 inches

12 inches

19 inches

Make a class supply of construction paper scarves of different lengths and invite each child to decorate one. Write the measurement of each scarf on a different construction paper hat cutout. Mount several of the scarves on the board along with a bird cutout (enlarge the pattern on page 95) and place the corresponding hats in a nearby container. A child measures each scarf and uses Sticky-Tac to attach the hat labeled with the corresponding measurement to each scarf.

Skating Into Winter Fun

My mom likes to <u>wrap</u> presents.

I want to play outside and <u>build</u> a snowman.

When I am cold, I like to <u>drink</u> hot chocolate.

We have a lot of fun when we <u>go</u> caroling.

My friends and I <u>sled</u> down the big hill.

My family and I <u>eat</u> a big Christmas dinner.

Sam and his family <u>light</u> their <u>menorah</u>.

Have each child use an assigned verb to write a sentence about a winter activity. Ask him to underline the verb and then illustrate the sentence. Mount the completed projects on a board along with an ice skate character (enlarge the pattern on page 96 and add a face).

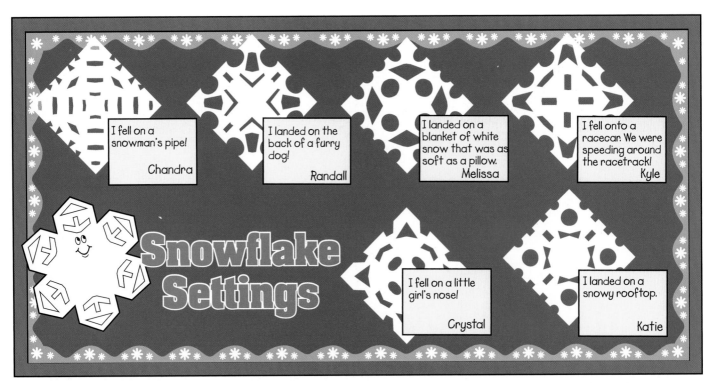

Post a snowflake character on a board (enlarge the pattern on page 97). Have each student fold an eight-inch white construction paper square in half four times to make a triangle and cut notches in it to make a snowflake. Then ask each child to imagine that she is a snowflake falling from the sky. Have her write on a blank card a sentence describing where she lands. Display each child's snowflake and card together.

Variations

- **A Flurry of Word Problems**
  Have each student make a paper snowflake; then lead students in counting the total number of snowflakes. Have each child write a word problem about snowflakes on a blank card, using the total number of snowflakes as one of the numbers in the problem. Post one problem a day on the board.

There were 26 snowflakes. 16 snowflakes melted. How many snowflakes were left?

- **A Snowflake's Journey**
  Have each student make a paper snowflake. Then ask each child to imagine that she is a snowflake. Invite her to write a story about her life. Mount each student's completed story with her snowflake.

Post a polar bear cutout (enlarge the pattern on page 98) on a wall near a paper fire. Have each child use a copy of page 99 to complete a book review of a book he has recently read. When he is finished with his review, have him cut it out. Post the completed book reviews around the polar bear.

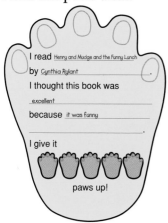

Use yarn to make four rows on the board. Label four blank cards each with a different snowy day activity and attach one card in each row. Have each student personalize a snowflake (pattern on page 97) and cut it out. Then ask each student to choose her favorite snowy day activity. Help each child attach her snowflake to the board in the corresponding row. Finally, discuss the results of the graph with the group. Incorporate the words *more, fewer, most, least,* and *equal* as appropriate.

Display these adorable penguins on a slippery iceberg along with student-generated penguin facts. After each child makes a penguin (see below), ask her to cut out a speech bubble and write a fact about penguins on it. Post each child's penguin along with her speech bubble.

Puffy Penguins

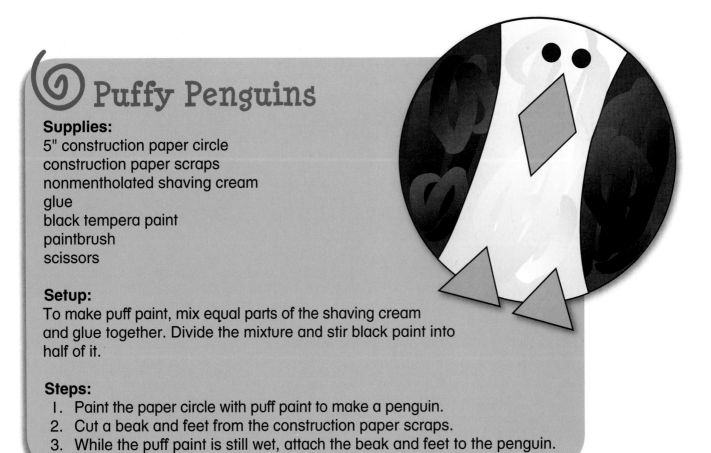

Supplies:
5" construction paper circle
construction paper scraps
nonmentholated shaving cream
glue
black tempera paint
paintbrush
scissors

Setup:
To make puff paint, mix equal parts of the shaving cream and glue together. Divide the mixture and stir black paint into half of it.

Steps:
1. Paint the paper circle with puff paint to make a penguin.
2. Cut a beak and feet from the construction paper scraps.
3. While the puff paint is still wet, attach the beak and feet to the penguin.

Post a few student-made tool cutouts on a board. Have each student make a snowpal shape and decorate it as desired. Then invite each child to write a description of how to build a snowpal. Display each child's snowpal and writing together.

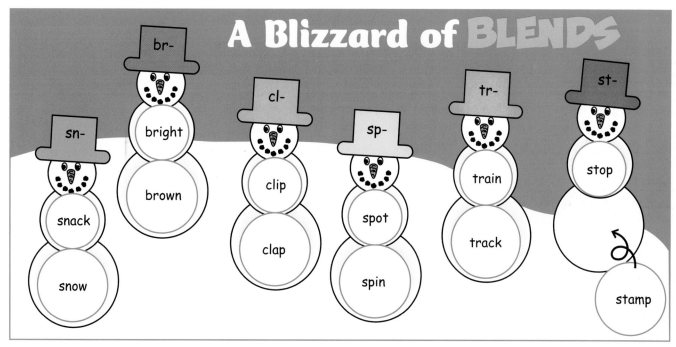

Cut snowy hills from white bulletin board paper and post them on a wall within student reach. Make a desired number of snowpal cutouts (pattern on page 100) and label each snowpal's hat with a different blend. Cut out a supply of white circles sized to match the snowpals' body parts and label each with a different word that begins with one of the featured blends. A child uses Sticky-Tac to attach each circle to the snowpal labeled with the corresponding blend.

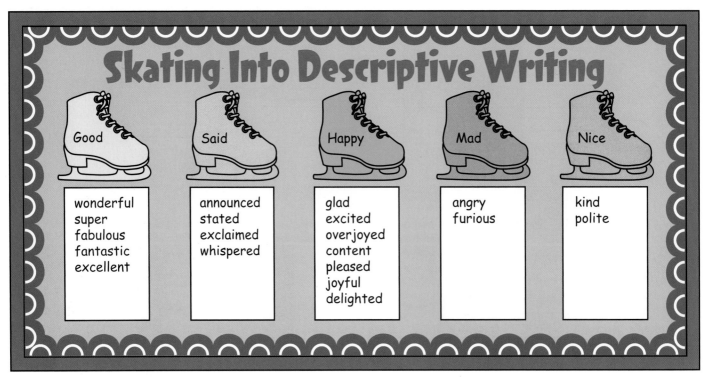

Skating Into Descriptive Writing

Good
wonderful
super
fabulous
fantastic
excellent

Said
announced
stated
exclaimed
whispered

Happy
glad
excited
overjoyed
content
pleased
joyful
delighted

Mad
angry
furious

Nice
kind
polite

Encourage students to use descriptive language with this simple display. Program several ice skate cutouts (pattern on page 96) each with a different overused word, such as *said*. Post each skate on a board above a strip of white bulletin board paper. Then have students brainstorm words that can be substituted for each overused word. List students' suggestions on each corresponding paper strip.

Student Activities

- **Alphabetical order:** Have each student choose one list of words. Then ask the child to rewrite his chosen list in alphabetical order.

- **Writing:** Have each student write a sentence using one of the overused words. Then have each child rewrite his sentence, substituting a more descriptive word for the overused word. Finally, invite each child to illustrate his new sentence.

Tyree
content
delighted
excited
glad
happy
joyful
overjoyed
pleased

Invite students to research record-setting cold temperatures in your area. Have children compare those temperatures to current and average monthly temperatures. Then ask each child to write about these temperature differences on a copy of a snowpal (pattern on page 100). Have each child color and cut out his snowpal when he is finished. Post the completed snowpals on a winter scene.

This display highlights Dr. Martin Luther King Jr.'s dream of peace. Ask students to think of a problem in their lives or in the world today. Then have each child write a description of the problem and a possible peaceful solution to the problem on copy of the dove pattern on page 97. After each student cuts out his dove, post the projects around an enlarged cutout of Dr. Martin Luther King Jr. (pattern on page 101).

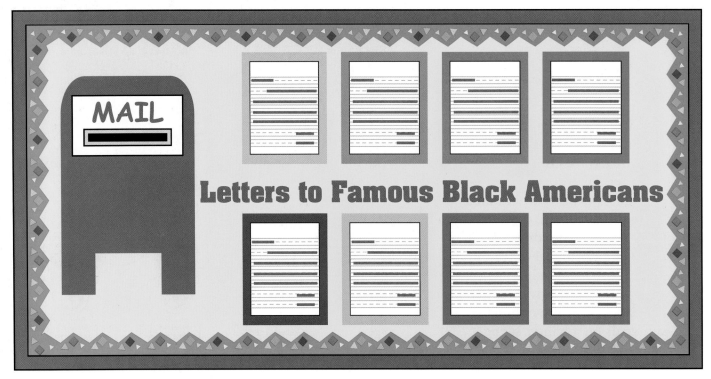

Celebrate Black History Month (February) with this display. Invite each student to research a prominent African American. Then have each student write a letter to his chosen person asking her a question or thanking her for a contribution to society. Have each child mount his work atop a slightly larger piece of construction paper and display the completed letters on a board along with a mailbox cutout.

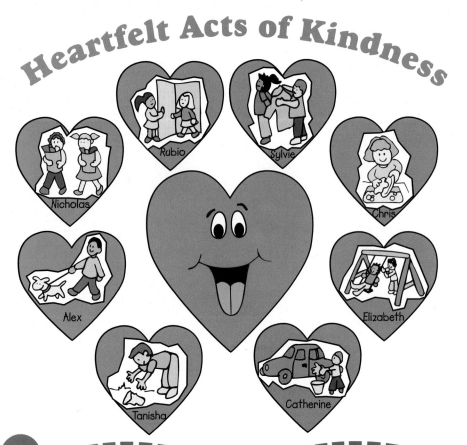

Invite students to look through discarded magazines and cut out pictures of someone demonstrating an act of kindness (or draw pictures illustrating an act of kindness). Have each student trim her picture and glue it to a personalized heart cutout. Post the completed hearts with an enlarged copy of the heart character on page 102.

Spring

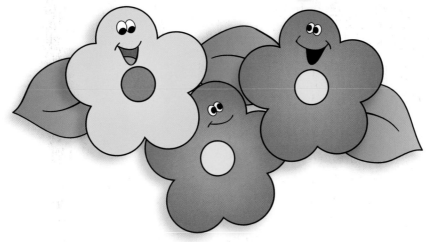

A dandelion is just a weed, or is it? Have each student write a descriptive sentence about a dandelion on a yellow triangle. Arrange the triangles along with a construction paper stem and leaves into a dandelion shape. Next, have each child write a wish on a white triangle. Arrange the triangles along with a construction paper stem to form a second dandelion.

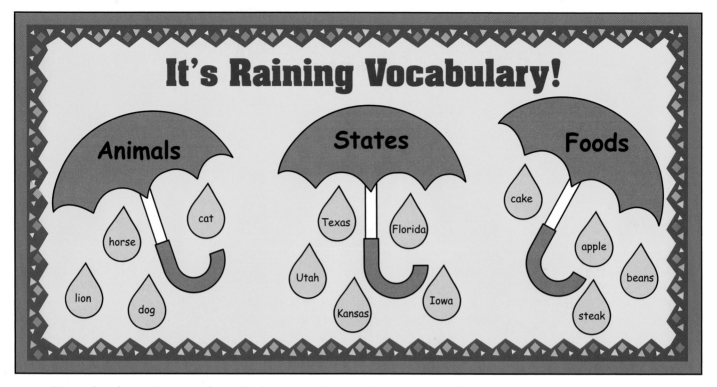

It's Raining Vocabulary!

To make this rainy weather display, post three enlarged umbrella cutouts (pattern on page 103) on a board. Program each umbrella with a different category. Place a supply of raindrop cutouts near the board. Invite each student to choose a category, write a related word on a raindrop cutout, and post the cutout under the matching umbrella.

✳ Variations

- **It's Raining Multisyllable Words!**
  Program each umbrella with a different number from 2 to 4. Have each student choose a number, write a word with that number of syllables on a raindrop cutout, and post the cutout under the matching umbrella.

- **It's Raining Long-Vowel Sounds!**
  Program each umbrella with a different vowel. Have each student choose a vowel, write on a raindrop cutout a word with that long-vowel sound, and post the cutout under the matching umbrella.

- **It's Raining Units of Measurement!**
  Program each umbrella with a different form of measurement. For example, write "weight" on the first umbrella, "length" on the second, and "capacity" on the third. Have each student choose a form of measurement, write a related unit of measure on a raindrop cutout, and post the cutout under the matching umbrella.

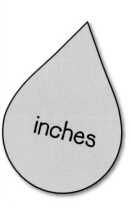

Program each of several cloud cutouts with a letter and a different math fact and then post the clouds on a board. Next, program a corresponding number of leaf cutouts each with a number that matches one of the math facts. Direct each child who visits the board to letter his paper, copy the math fact that goes with each letter, and then write the number that answers the math fact.

March may come in like a lion and go out like a lamb, but are there other ways to describe the wild weather associated with this month? Direct each student to write her ideas, along with the sentence starters shown, on a sheet of paper; then have her illustrate her work. Display the completed projects so that everyone can enjoy the new images of March weather!

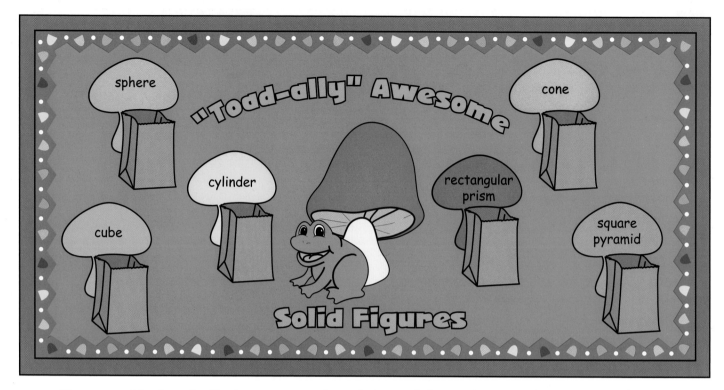

To create this shapely display, post an enlarged copy of the toad pattern from page 104 on the board. Next, program six mushrooms each with a different name of a solid figure and then attach each mushroom to the board. On each mushroom, staple a brown lunch bag. Instruct students to place real-life examples, or pictures of examples, of each solid figure in the bags. Periodically remove the examples and discuss them with the class.

Give each student a copy of the bee pattern on page 105. Direct the child to write on the bee's wing an adjective that describes spring. Display the completed bees around a large construction paper flower.

All turtles lay their eggs on land.

One type of turtle may lay 200 eggs at a time.

Many animals try to eat turtle eggs.

Look Who's Hatching

Mount an enlarged copy of the basket pattern from page 106 on a board. Have each child trim a folded sheet of 9" x 12" white construction paper into an egg shape so that it makes a booklet that opens on the fold. On the cover of his booklet, have the child draw and color a picture of an animal that hatches from an egg. On the inside, have the child write facts about the animal. Post the eggs on the board.

Use the basket again. See page 40.

Student Activities

- **Comparing and contrasting:** A student creates a Venn diagram about two animals from the board.

- **Writing a paragraph:** A student writes a paragraph about one animal that's featured on the display.

- **Solving story problems:** On the front of an index card, a student writes a story problem about one or two animals from the board. On the back of the card, the student writes the answer. Collect the cards and place them in a learning center.

One alligator lays three eggs. Another alligator lays four eggs. How many eggs do the alligators lay in all?

Have small groups of students use construction paper and yarn to create the four stages of a plant's life cycle across the bottom of the board. On one side of the board, mount several raindrops. On the other side, mount a large sun cutout.

For this rich story display, mount a large pot of gold on a board. Trim a class supply of writing paper into circles and then give one piece to each child. On the paper, have the child write a story about finding a leprechaun's pot of gold. Then have him mount the paper on a yellow sheet of construction paper and trim the yellow paper to create a border.

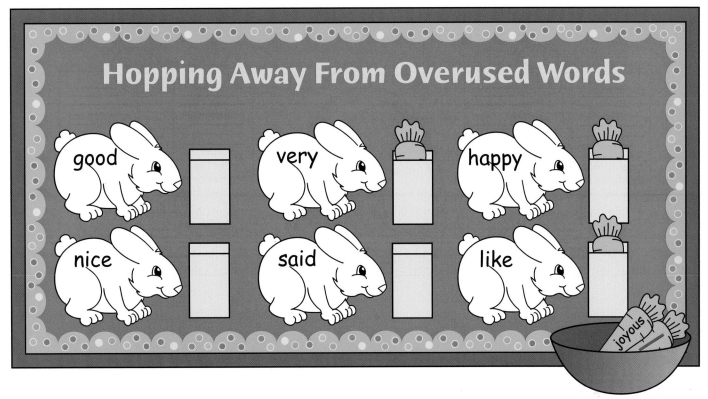

Hopping Away From Overused Words

Program each of several rabbit cutouts (pattern on page 107) with a different overused word. Mount the rabbits on the board. Staple a library pocket beside each rabbit. In addition, program several carrot cutouts (pattern on page 107) each with a different word that matches one of the overused words. Store the carrots near the board. A child reads the word on each carrot and then places the carrot in the corresponding library pocket.

Variations

- **Hopping Into Math Facts**
  Program each rabbit cutout with a different number. In addition, program several carrot cutouts each with a different math fact whose answer is on a rabbit.

- **Hopping Into Contractions**
  Program each rabbit cutout with a different contraction. Then, program several pairs of carrot cutouts each with a different pair of words that make one of the contractions on the rabbits.

Post an enlarged copy of the basket pattern from page 106 on the board along with a few paper eggs. Have each student personalize and decorate an egg-shaped cutout. After each student has chosen a sample of his best work, mount the work along with the decorated eggs. Periodically ask students to replace their displayed work with other samples.

Use the basket again. See page 37.

Staple a large Earth cutout to a bulletin board. Have students help you collect and tack clean pieces of litter to the cutout. Then post an enlarged cutout of the clutter bug pattern on page 108 on the board.

Attach a large jar-shaped cutout to the door. Each week use Sticky-Tac to place a card with a new number at the top of the jar. Give each student a jelly bean–shaped cutout (pattern on page 108) and have her write a number sentence on the cutout that equals the number on the display. Then have her use Sticky-Tac to place her cutout on the jar. Make extra cutouts available so that students can add to the display throughout the week.

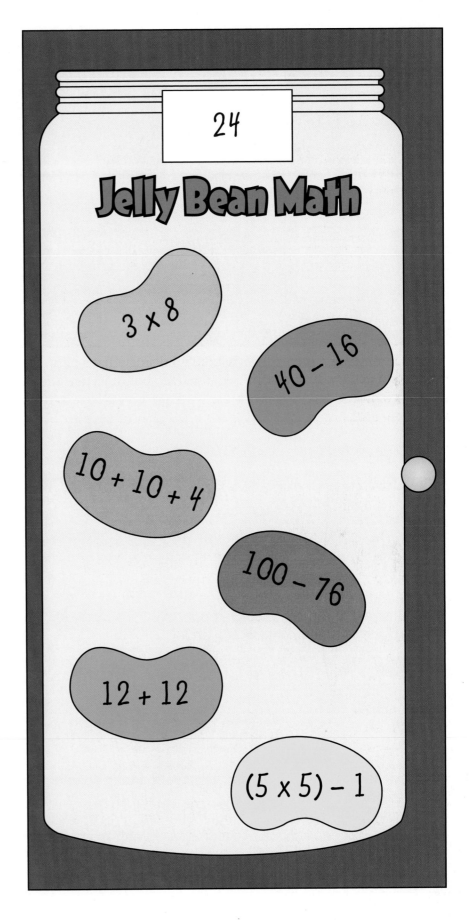

24

Jelly Bean Math

3 x 8

40 – 16

10 + 10 + 4

100 – 76

12 + 12

(5 x 5) – 1

Just in time for Cinco de Mayo, here's a display that's peppered with students' best work. Have each child make a string of hot peppers (see below). Then staple the strings on a board around examples of students' best work.

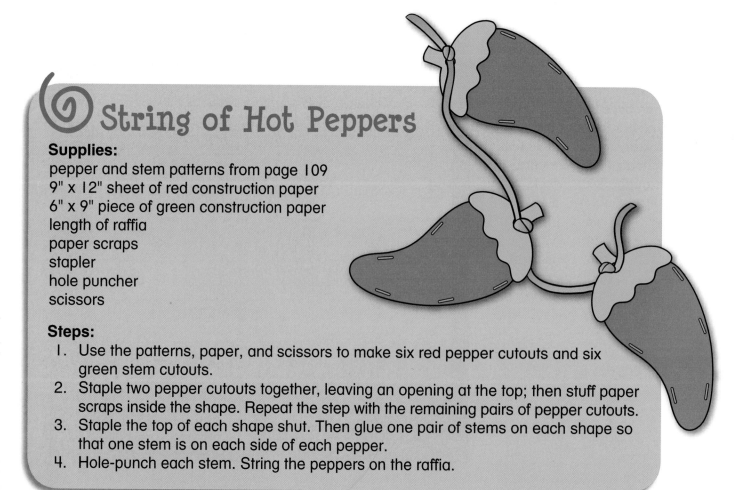

String of Hot Peppers

Supplies:
pepper and stem patterns from page 109
9" x 12" sheet of red construction paper
6" x 9" piece of green construction paper
length of raffia
paper scraps
stapler
hole puncher
scissors

Steps:
1. Use the patterns, paper, and scissors to make six red pepper cutouts and six green stem cutouts.
2. Staple two pepper cutouts together, leaving an opening at the top; then stuff paper scraps inside the shape. Repeat the step with the remaining pairs of pepper cutouts.
3. Staple the top of each shape shut. Then glue one pair of stems on each shape so that one stem is on each side of each pepper.
4. Hole-punch each stem. String the peppers on the raffia.

Celebrate Cinco de Mayo by highlighting Spanish vocabulary! On each of several bear character cutouts (pattern on page 110), write a different English word. Then staple the cutouts on a bulletin board. Next, write the Spanish word for each English word on a different sombrero cutout (pattern on page 110) and place the sombrero cutouts near the bulletin board. A child uses Sticky-Tac to place each sombrero on the matching bear.

Give each pair of students a copy of the butterfly pattern on page 111. Direct the pair to write an assigned vowel sound on the butterfly's body. Then have the pair work together to write four words that each have the assigned vowel sound, one on each section of the butterfly's wings. Provide assorted craft materials—such as watercolor paints, sequins, and pom-poms—and have each pair decorate its butterfly as desired.

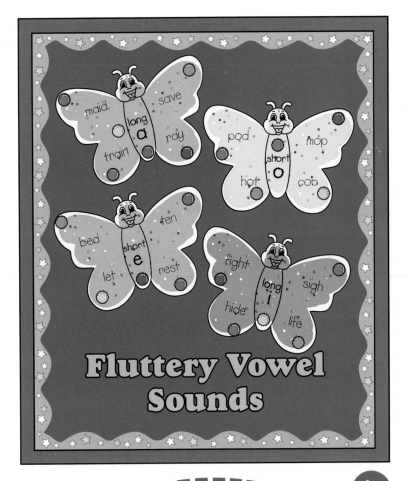

Flowerful Fractions

Have each student use different colors of construction paper to create a flower that represents a fraction. Then have her program a paper circle with a fraction that matches the flower. Display the flowers on the board.

Our "Berry" Favorite Homophones

Make several strawberry-shaped cutouts (pattern on page 77). Program each strawberry with a pair of homophones and then cut the strawberry in half. Mount one-half of each strawberry on the wall and place the other strawberry halves in a container nearby. A student matches each strawberry half to the half with the matching homophone.

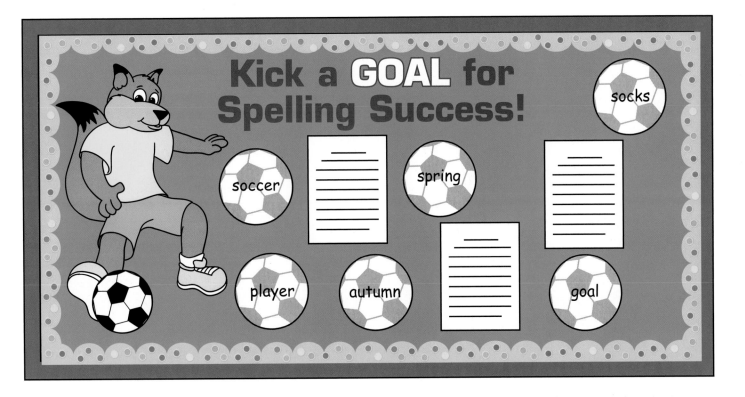

Program a set of laminated soccer ball cutouts each with a different spelling word. Mount the cutouts, enlarged soccer player character (pattern on page 112), and the title on a board. Throughout the week, post examples of students' best spelling work on the board. Each week, wipe off the cutouts and write the new week's spelling words on them.

Student Activities

- **Writing sentences:** A student writes sentences that each include a different spelling word.

- **Parts of speech:** A student writes each spelling word and then underlines it with a different-colored crayon according to the color code:
    nouns = blue
    verbs = red
    adjectives = green
    adverbs = orange

- **Writing a story:** A student writes a story about playing a soccer game. He uses at least four of the words from the display in his story.

Post several pond-shaped cutouts. Program several cards each with a different type of poetry and post one card above each pond. Have each child write an original poem on a duck-shaped cutout (pattern on page 113). Then enlist students' help in posting the cutouts in the appropriate pond.

Here's the Scoop!

This flavorful display builds students' self-esteem *and* helps them set goals! Give each child three copies of the scoop pattern on page 109. Have the child copy and complete the sentence starters shown on each scoop. Then have her cut a cone out of brown construction paper. Next, have her assemble her ice-cream cone and post it on the wall.

End of the Year

To make this bright display, post an enlarged sun cutout (pattern on page 114). Have each student write an assigned word on a yellow construction paper circle (sun). Then have him program several yellow construction paper strips (rays) each with a different synonym of the featured word. Mount his sun and rays together on the wall.

Armfuls of Math

Have each student label a copy of the octopus pattern on page 115 with an assigned number. Next, have her list on each of her octopus's arms a different math problem that has the featured number as its answer. Then invite her to color and cut out her octopus. Mount the completed projects on a board.

✳ Variations

- **Armfuls of Word Families**
  Have each child write an assigned rime on an octopus cutout. Then have her write a different word containing the featured rime on each of her octopus's arms.

- **Armfuls of Fun in Third Grade**
  Have each student personalize an octopus cutout. Then have her write on each of the octopus's arms one thing she learned this school year. Have each child color her octopus. Invite each student, in turn, to share her octopus with the class.

Jump Into Parts of Speech

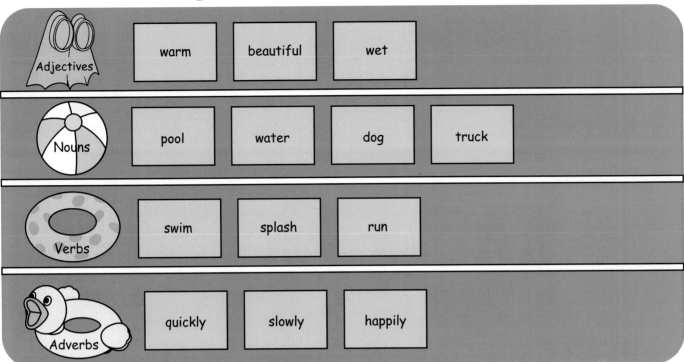

This display gives students practice with parts of speech. Draw four lanes on a pool shape cut from blue bulletin board paper. Label each of the pool toy cutouts (patterns on page 116) with a different part of speech and mount each in a different lane. Write a few words from each of the featured parts of speech, each on a separate blank card. A child uses Sticky-Tac to attach each card in the appropriate lane.

Direct each student to write a paragraph about what he expects will happen in the next grade level. Then have him illustrate his paragraph on a crystal ball cutout (pattern on page 117). Have him drizzle glue over his picture and sprinkle clear glitter on the glue. After the glue dries, have the child shake off the excess glitter. Display each student's crystal ball along with his paragraph.

Scrapbook of Success

Display students' achievements from the school year on an oversize scrapbook page. To make the page, fold a length of bulletin board paper in half; then unfold it to reveal a crease in the middle of the paper. Have each youngster write about something he achieved during the school year, illustrate his writing, and then glue his work to a colorful piece of scrapbook paper. Display youngsters' completed projects on the scrapbook page.

Complete and post on a board an enlarged copy of the director's clapboard (pattern on page 118). Direct each child to write about and illustrate three highlights from the school year on a copy of the filmstrip shape (pattern on page 117). Staple the filmstrips around the director's clapboard.

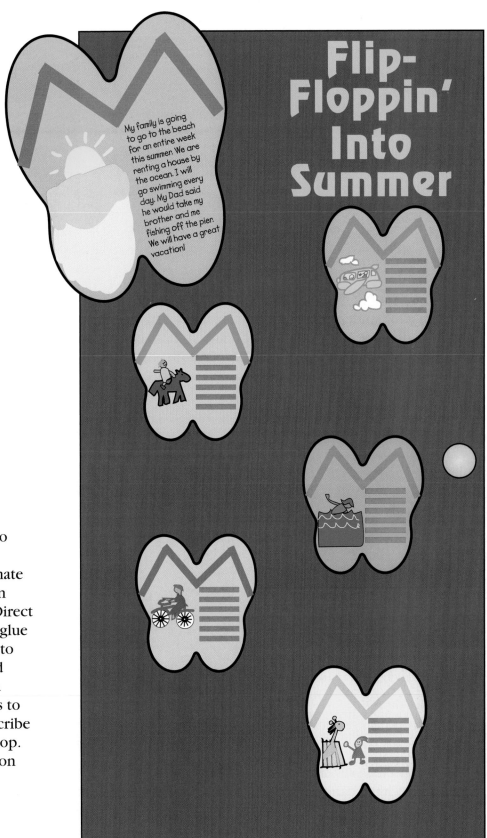

Flip-Floppin' Into Summer

My family is going to go to the beach for an entire week this summer. We are renting a house by the ocean. I will go swimming every day. My Dad said he would take my brother and me fishing off the pier. We will have a great vacation!

Invite students to jump into summer with both feet! Have each child work with a classmate to trace on a sheet of paper an outline of his shoe-clad feet. Direct him to cut out the shape and glue ribbon pieces to it, as shown, to make flip-flops. Have the child draw on one of his flip-flops a picture of something he plans to do this summer and then describe his picture on the other flip-flop. Post the completed flip-flops on your classroom door.

Give your students a send-off that reaches new heights! Post an enlarged airplane cutout (pattern on page 119) on a piece of blue bulletin board paper. Have each student personalize a cloud shape she has cut from a sheet of white construction paper. Then have her glue to her cloud a photo of herself. Post the clouds by the airplane.

Attach a large hand cutout to a board. Then ask each student to trace around his hand on colorful paper and cut out the tracing. Have each child write on a blank card a message he would like to share with next year's students. Post each student's handprint on the board along with his card. Keep the board intact throughout the summer so that it will be ready to share with your new students at the beginning of the next school year.

Anytime

Wash Day the ABC Way

cake candy cookies doughnuts pie sorbet

Secure a length of yarn across a wall. Write a different word on each of several T-shirt cutouts (pattern on page 120). To make the display self-checking, number the back of each shirt to show the correct ABC order of the words. Place the prepared shirts and several clothespins in a basket by the clothesline. A child hangs the shirts in alphabetical order on the line.

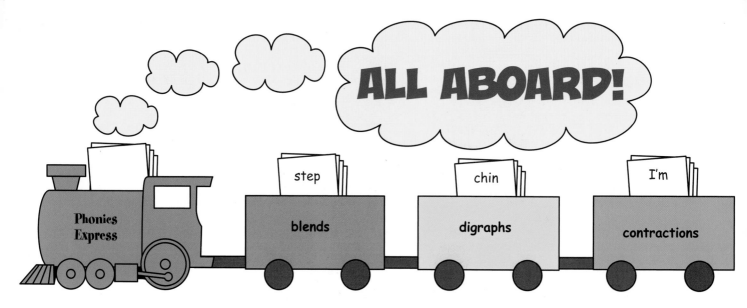

Post an enlarged copy of the engine pattern from page 121. Make three train cars and then program each one with a different one of the following words: *blends, contractions,* or *digraphs.* Mount the train cars so that each one creates a pocket. Program a desired number of index cards, each with a different word that matches one of the descriptions. Store the cards in a container near the board. A student places each card in the matching train car.

Have each child color and cut out a copy of the banana pattern on page 122. Then have him write on a card an adjective that describes his banana. Showcase each banana with its corresponding card next to an enlarged colored copy of the monkey pattern on page 123. Next, post a laminated sentence strip along the bottom of the board. Each day, invite a different student to use a wipe-off marker to write on the sentence strip a sentence that includes at least one of the displayed adjectives.

Spotlight on Synonyms

Synonyms are words with similar meanings.

hot — burning, searing, fiery, roasting

nice — pleasant, agreeable

happy — cheerful, joyous, glad

walk — stroll, amble, promenade

tired — weary, worn-out

sad — gloomy, dispirited

For each student, program a copy of the flashlight pattern on page 122 with a different word. Have the child color and cut out the flashlight. Then have her write synonyms for her word on paper rectangles (beams of light). Post the flashlights and beams on a board along with an enlarged copy of the dog pattern on page 80.

Use the dog again. See page 9.

✳ Variations

- **Spotlight on Safety!**
  Have each student write on a card a safety rule for fire prevention, Halloween, bike riding, or another timely topic. Glue the cards to a large paper circle (spotlight). Then post personalized flashlights around the rules.

- **Beaming With Student Responsibility!**
  Write different classroom jobs on individual flashlight cutouts. Have each student personalize a paper rectangle. To assign jobs, place a student's beam by the corresponding flashlight.

- **"Who's" Beaming?**
  Have each student personalize a flashlight pattern to post on the board. Then have him write on rectangular paper strips three sentences about himself without using his name. Each week, display one child's sentences, lead the class to determine who the beams describe, and move the corresponding flashlight to feature that student.

Paper passers — Christy, Jamal

Line leader — Parker

Far-out Word Families

Program an enlarged spaceship cutout (pattern on page 125) with a desired word family and then post the spaceship on a board. Have each child make a martian (see below). Then have him program the index card on his martian with words that contain the featured word family. Attach the completed martians to the board.

Crafty Martian

Supplies:
sheet of construction paper
paper scraps
craft materials
index cards
scissors
glue
access to a stapler

Steps:
1. Staple an index card to the sheet of construction paper.
2. Trim the paper to your liking to create the martian's body.
3. Use paper scraps and craft materials to add details to the martian.

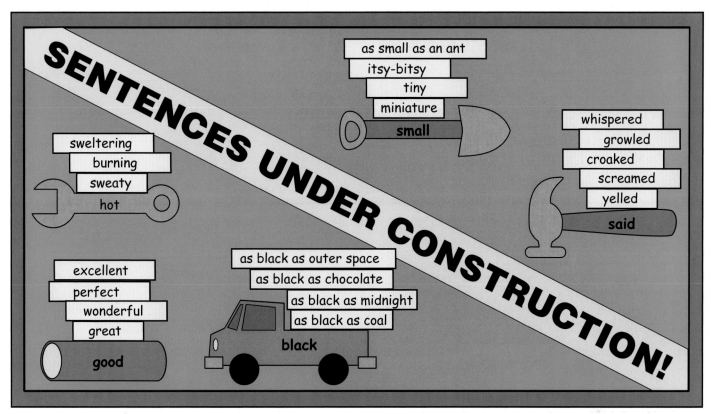

Make several construction-related items and program each one with a different overused word. Staple the items to a board. As a class, brainstorm words or phrases that can replace each overused word. Write students' responses on paper strips and then post each strip above its matching item.

After a child reads a book, have him choose a character that deserves an award. The child completes a copy of the award (page 126), colors it, and cuts it out. Post the completed awards by an enlarged colored copy of the owl pattern (page 124).

Use the owl again. See page 59.

Puzzle Prompts

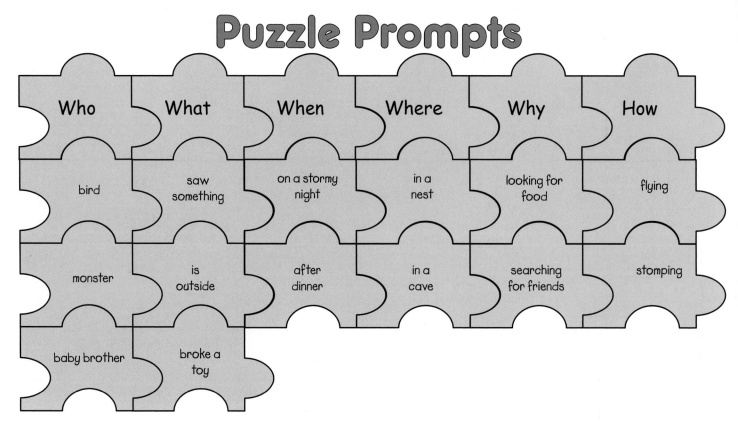

Who	What	When	Where	Why	How
bird	saw something	on a stormy night	in a nest	looking for food	flying
monster	is outside	after dinner	in a cave	searching for friends	stomping
baby brother	broke a toy				

On different puzzle pieces (pattern on page 127), write the following words: *Who, What, When, Where, Why,* and *How.* Post the interlocking pieces on a wall. Give each small group of students six copies of the puzzle piece pattern. Direct the group to program each piece with an example of a different story element. Build the wall puzzle by interlocking the pieces below the matching headings. Encourage students to refer to it as they write realistic or silly stories.

Westward Wagons!

As the class reads a historical fiction book aloud, have each student write a summary of each chapter. Each day, invite several students to trim individual index cards so that they resemble the top of a covered wagon. On his card, have a child copy his chapter summary. Then have him use construction paper scraps to complete his covered wagon. Post the wagons on the board. Each day, have different students make covered wagons to add to the train. To complete the display, write the book's title on a flag cutout and staple it to the lead wagon.

To prepare this prediction-filled display, post an enlarged copy of the owl (pattern on page 124) and a book cutout labeled with a desired book title. Post a large speech bubble cutout labeled as shown. Next, read aloud the book without reading the ending. Give each child a sheet of paper and have her write her prediction for the ending of the story. Post students' work on the board.

Use the owl again. See page 57.

Student Activities

- **Write a response:** Have each student select one paper displayed on the board. Direct him to write a letter to respond to the author of the paper.

- **Conduct an interview:** Pair children and have them share their work before they post it. Then instruct each child to develop interview questions based on her partner's work.

- **Compare and contrast:** Have each student select a paper on the board to compare with his own work. Then have him create a Venn diagram to record the similarities and differences between the two papers.

Dear Mary,
   I thought it would have been nice if Bardy visited the family too. It's nice that Bardy is free, but if it were me, I would still want to have him around in the house.
                    From,
                    Harry

Suffix Swimmers

Guide each student to write a root word on the bottom of a copy of the fishbowl pattern on page 128. Instruct her to color and cut out the fishbowl. Next, have her write related words using different suffixes on individual fish cutouts and then glue each fish to her fishbowl. Post the completed crafts for a "fin-tastic" reference display!

✴ Variations

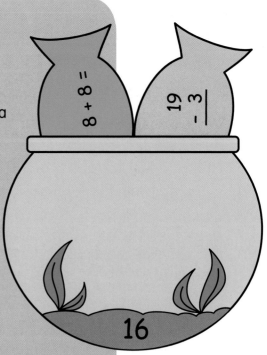

- **Factual Fish?**
  Post two enlarged copies of the fishbowl pattern. Write "fact" on one bowl and "opinion" on the other. Then have each student write a fish-related fact on a fish cutout and a fish-related opinion on a second fish. Then have her post each cutout on the matching fishbowl.

- **Fishy Facts!**
  Label individual fishbowls with desired sums and differences. Staple each fishbowl to a board so that it forms a pocket. Then program large fish cutouts with corresponding math problems. A youngster solves each problem and then slides the fish into the fishbowl with the correct answer.

- **Fish Friends**
  Have each student write his name on a fish cutout and glue it to a fishbowl. Post the completed projects on a board and encourage students to catch each other performing random acts of kindness. When a good deed is observed, reward the child who was caught by feeding (sprinkling pretend food at the top of his bowl) his fish.

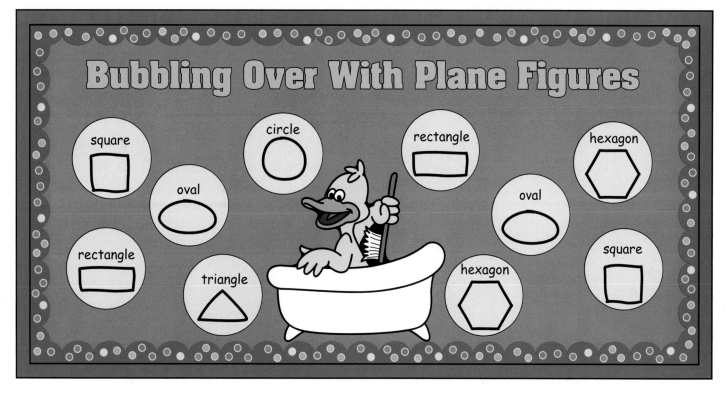

Bubbling Over With Plane Figures

square

circle

rectangle

hexagon

oval

oval

rectangle

triangle

hexagon

square

Post on a board an enlarged copy of the duck pattern on page 129. Program a class supply of bubble-shaped cutouts with the names of plane figures. Distribute the cutouts and instruct each child to draw his assigned shape on his cutout. Collect the cutouts and staple them to the board.

To create this display, program each of four enlarged cookie jar cutouts (pattern on page 130) with a different multiplication product. Post the cutouts on a board. Next, program several cookie-shaped cutouts each with a different multiplication problem that equals one of the featured products. Display the cookies near the board. A student uses Sticky-Tac to match each cookie to the appropriate jar.

Cookie Computation

6 x 3 =

2 x 9 =

18

2 x 18 =

6 x 6 =

12 x 3 =

36

4 x 6 =

12 x 2 =

8 x 3 =

6 x 4 =

24

1 x 64 =

8 x 8 =

64

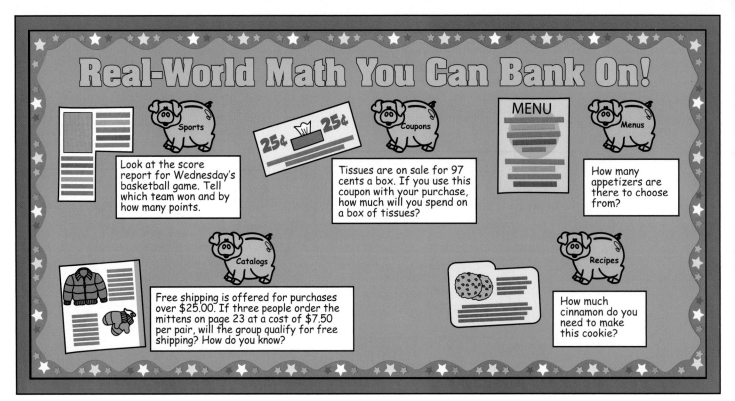

Real-World Math You Can Bank On!

Sports: Look at the score report for Wednesday's basketball game. Tell which team won and by how many points.

Coupons: Tissues are on sale for 97 cents a box. If you use this coupon with your purchase, how much will you spend on a box of tissues?

Menus: How many appetizers are there to choose from?

Catalogs: Free shipping is offered for purchases over $25.00. If three people order the mittens on page 23 at a cost of $7.50 per pair, will the group qualify for free shipping? How do you know?

Recipes: How much cinnamon do you need to make this cookie?

Write the name of each category shown on an individual tagboard pig cutout (pattern on page 131). Make a slit in each cutout (coin slot) and then staple three of its edges to a board to create a pocket. Post a corresponding math problem and a real-world item with each pig. A student answers each question on a copy of the recording sheet on page 131. For each correct answer, she inserts a paper circle (coin) into the corresponding piggy bank.

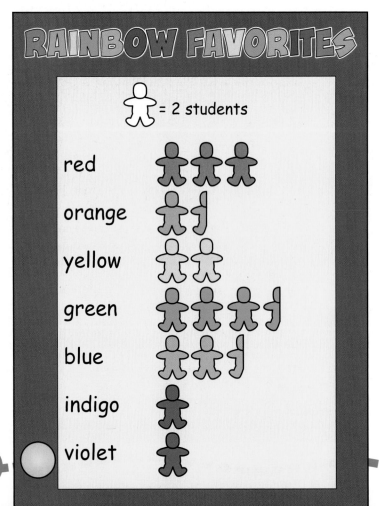

To prepare this door display, write the colors of the rainbow in a column on a large sheet of paper. Make a key that shows that a person cutout (patterns on page 132) equals two students. Then have each child color a copy of the person pattern on page 132 to show his favorite color of the rainbow. Lead students to sort the completed patterns to complete the graph. After the cutouts are glued to the graph, use the resulting display to make favorite color comparisons.

Send the message that math rules with this display. Have each student label a 2" x 12" strip of yellow paper so it resembles a ruler. After he adds cutout features, post the ruler on the board with a sample of his best math work.

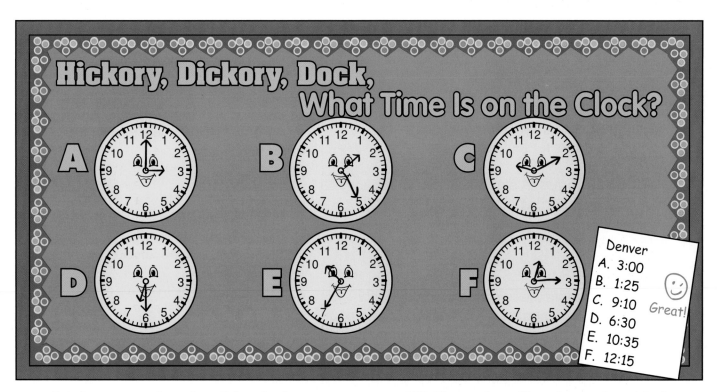

Laminate several copies of the clock pattern on page 133. Use a wipe-off marker to draw clock hands on each clock to display different times. Post each completed clock on a board next to an identifying letter. A student records each clock's time on a sheet of paper.

Review shapes with these creative cats! Have each student use an assortment of construction paper shapes to make a cat. Encourage him to use crayons or markers to add details. Then have him write on a card the names of the shapes he used. Post each completed cat with the corresponding card.

Student Activities

- **Writing simple instructions:** A student writes the steps for making his cat.

- **Writing dialogue:** A student selects another cat from the board and writes a conversation the cat could have with his cat. He punctuates the conversation correctly.

- **Descriptive writing:** A student writes descriptive sentences about one of the cats on the display. Then he reads his sentences aloud and his classmates guess which cat he is describing.

Tristan's Feline Figure

You will need
1 large circle
2 small circles
2 large ovals
2 small ovals
2 large rectangles
2 small triangles
glue
markers

Directions:
1. Glue two rectangles side by side behind the large circle to make front legs.
2. Glue a large oval to the outside of each leg to make back legs.
3. Glue a small circle to the bottom of each front leg to make front paws.
4. Glue a small oval to the bottom of each back leg to make back paws.
5. Glue two triangles to the top of the large circle to make ears.
6. Use markers to make a face.

Mathematical Munchies

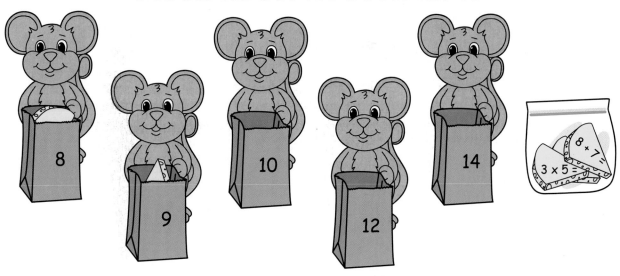

Write math facts on cheese cutouts (pattern on page 134) that correspond with answers that have been programmed on paper bags. Staple each bag to a mouse cutout (pattern on page 135). Arrange the mice and desired embellishments on a wall. A student takes a cheese cutout, solves the problem, and drops it into the corresponding bag.

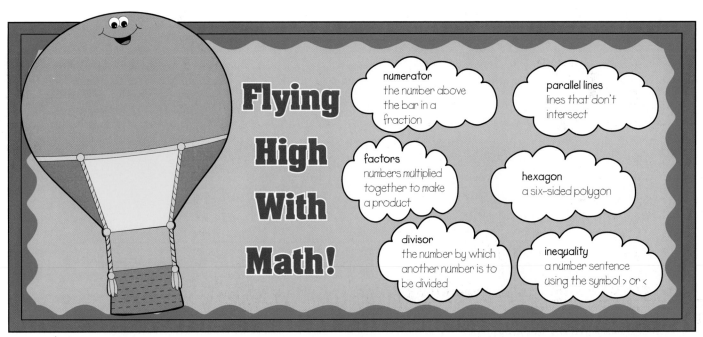

Reinforce math vocabulary with a reusable display! Laminate several cloud cutouts and mount them on a board with an enlarged copy of the hot-air balloon pattern on page 136. Label each cloud with a different math term. Invite students to write a definition for each posted word. Then use a wipe-off marker to write the student-generated definitions. As youngsters learn new words, add more clouds or wipe off the displayed ones and use them again!

Program three sets of ten bee cutouts (pattern on page 105) each with a different number from 0 to 9. Then staple six beehive-shaped cutouts on a board. Next, write several multiple-digit numbers, in expanded form, on sentence strips. Staple the bottom edge and two sides of each strip on the board next to a beehive. A student uses the programmed bees to form each number by sliding the bees into the sentence strip.

 Variations

- **Homophone Hives**
  On each of two bees, write a word to make a homophone pair. Then program a beehive with a sentence using one of the words, leaving a blank for the homophone. Continue in this manner to make more homophone-related sentences. A student matches the correct word to complete each sentence.

- **Ordered Insects**
  Write a different number on each of several beehive cutouts. Then post a laminated bee on each side of each hive. A child writes the number that comes before and after each posted number.

- **Bee Buddies**
  Write each student's name on an individual bee cutout. Each week, post the bees in pairs or small groups to assign partners or groups.

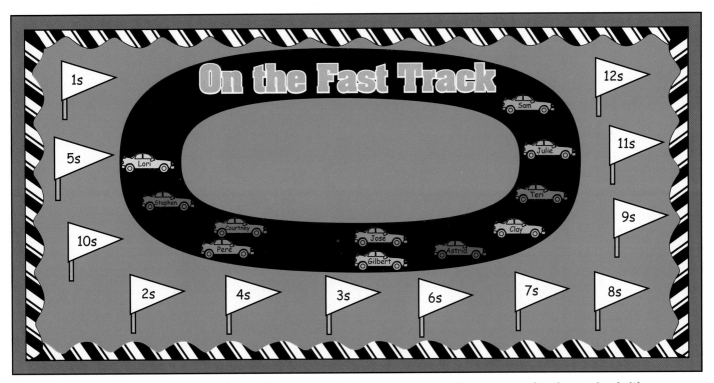

Students master multiplication tables to move these racecars! Decorate a display to look like a racetrack. Label signs and flags around the track with different times tables. Then have each student color, cut out, and personalize a copy of a racecar pattern on page 140. As each child masters a table, move his car around the track to the next marker. The race is on!

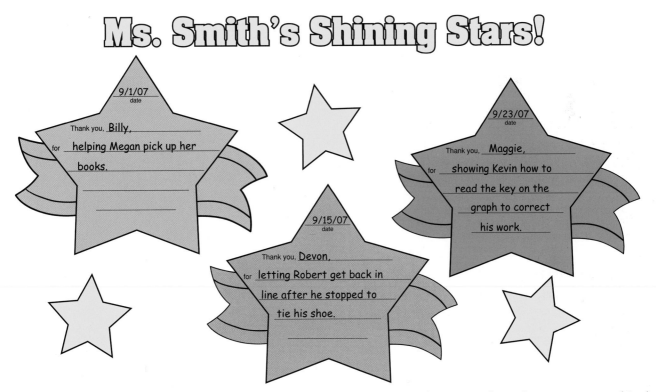

These stars are sure to prove that kindness is contagious! When a student demonstrates a kind act or a good deed, reward her with a construction paper star award (pattern on page 140) to showcase on the display. No doubt there will soon be a star-filled wall to be proud of!

"Moo-velous" Work

These cute cows are sure to call attention to super student work! Secure green fabric to a board to create a green pasture. After each child makes a cow (see below), encourage him to select an assignment that he is proud to post beside his cow. Periodically, provide opportunities for students to showcase a different work of excellence.

Spotted Cow

Supplies:
cow pattern on page 137
brown or black paper scraps
markers or crayons
scissors
glue

Steps:
1. Color the cow.
2. Tear the scraps into smaller pieces to make cow spots.
3. Glue the spots to your cow.
4. Cut out the cow.

We Are Right on Target!

Have each student color and cut out a copy of the bull's-eye and arrow patterns on page 138. Guide her to post her bull's-eye on the display. Have a child choose a piece of work of which she is proud and then attach her arrow and paper to the corresponding bull's-eye to show off her high score!

Dynamite Work!

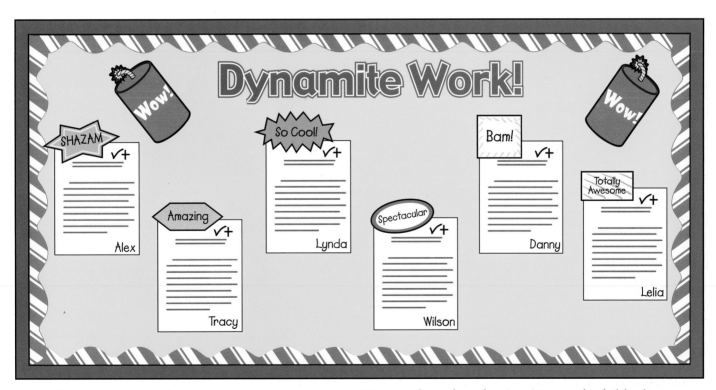

Post two firecracker cutouts (pattern on page 82) on a board as shown. Give each child a large card. Have him decorate the card with markers to feature a unique word or phrase that calls attention to an outstanding performance. Post his card atop a sampling of his exceptional work for a dynamic display!

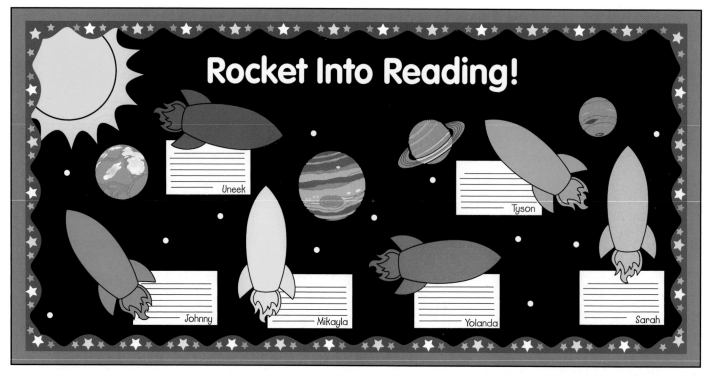

This book-review display is out of this world! Have each student color and cut out a copy of the rocket pattern on page 139. When a student finishes reading a book, have him write a description of the story on a card. Then post the rockets and cards on a board that's been decorated with an outer space theme.

Variations

- **Blasting Off With Great Work!**
  Have each student use craft materials to decorate a cardboard tube so that it resembles a rocket. Use the craft as a paper topper to showcase students' work.

- **Blast Off to Good Behavior!**
  When a student is caught making a good choice, move his rocket toward a posted goal on the display. When each child reaches the goal, reward his positive behavior with a treat or special privilege.

- **To the Moon With Math!**
  Display each rocket as a paper topper for outstanding math assignments. If desired, write a featured math skill on a large moon-shaped cutout.

Program an enlarged sea animal cutout (pattern on page 141) with a different individual or class goal. Decorate a door with an underwater scene and post the cutouts there. When a goal is achieved, have each youngster color, cut out, and personalize a copy of the corresponding pattern to add to the display. Each visitor to your classroom is sure to be impressed by your super swimmers!

Multiplication memorized for 3s

Fernando

Tamika

Kim

All lunchroom rules followed for five days in a row

Melony

Read a chapter book

Marguerite

Kevin

Seaworthy Students

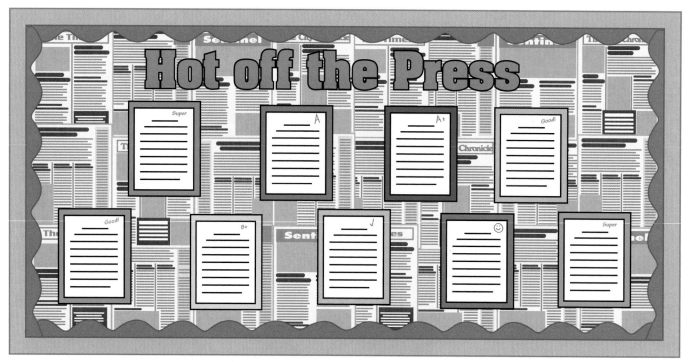

Hot off the Press

Display students' best work with this easy-to-make display! Cover a bulletin board with newspaper; then add the title and a border. Post samples of students' best work atop sheets of colorful construction paper.

Here's a quick and easy way to display classroom jobs! Label each petal of a large flower cutout with a classroom job. Then have each student color, cut out, and personalize a copy of the bee pattern on page 105. Tack a bee by each petal to assign a student to each job. Tack extra bee helpers to the center of the flower. Each week, move the bees around the flower to rotate helping hands.

Happy Birthday!

January

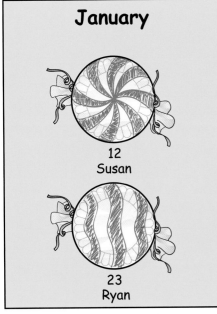

12
Susan

23
Ryan

February

16
Seth

March

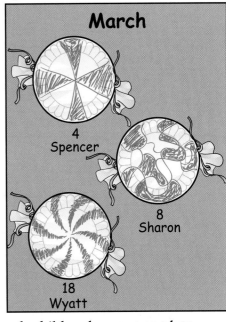

4
Spencer

8
Sharon

18
Wyatt

Add a sweet touch to your birthday board with this craft! Have each child make a paper plate candy (see below). Post each completed treat to display students' birthdays. On a child's birthday, invite each classmate to write a sweet message on a paper plate–size circle. Unwrap the child's plate, staple the meaningful messages between the decorated plate and a second plate, and rewrap the craft. Present the sentiment-filled candy to the child.

Paper Plate Candy

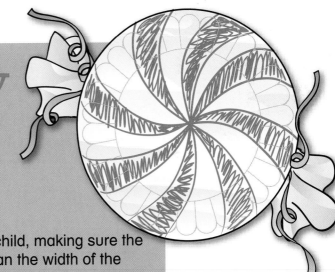

Supplies:
small paper plate
cellophane
2 lengths of ribbon
markers

Setup:
Measure two lengths of cellophane for each child, making sure the length of each piece is eight inches longer than the width of the plate.

Steps:
1. Draw a design on the back of the plate so that it resembles a piece of candy.
2. Place long pieces of cellophane atop and beneath the plate.
3. Use ribbon to tie each end of surplus cellophane together so that it resembles a candy wrapper. (The plate will be secure inside the wrapper.)

Crow Pattern
Use with "A Sweet Slice of Summer" on page 5.

TEC61093

TEC61093

Dumbbell Pattern
Use with "Feeling Fit for Second Grade" on page 6.

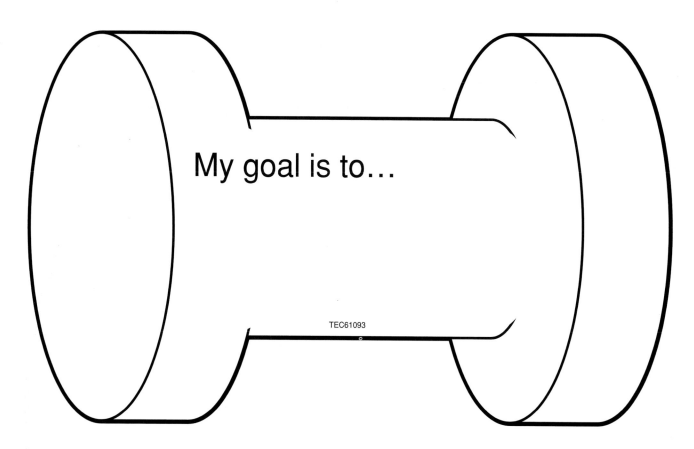

My goal is to…

TEC61093

Fish Pattern
Use with "Reeling in a Good Catch" on page 7 and "Diving Into a New School Year" on page 10.

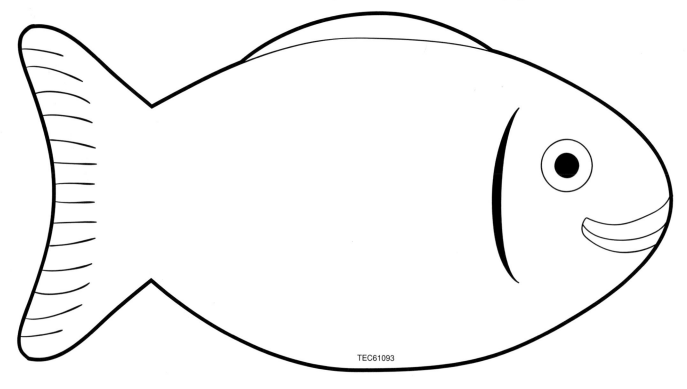

TEC61093

Use with "It's 'Berry' Nice to Meet You!" on page 6 and "Our 'Berry' Favorite Homophones" on page 44.

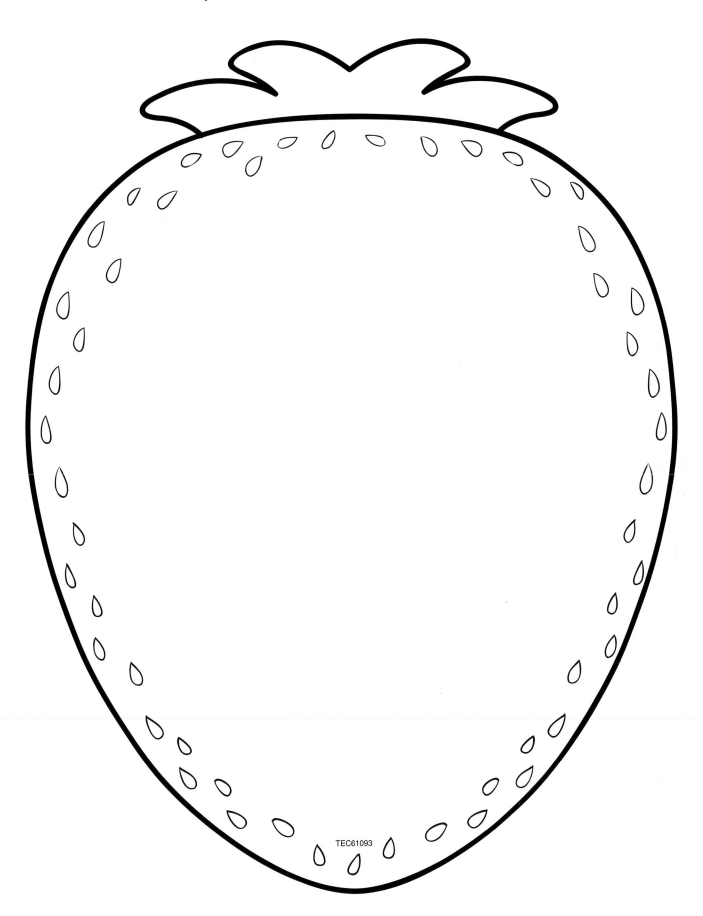

TEC61093

Tiger Pattern

Use with "Reeling in a Good Catch" on page 7.

TEC61093

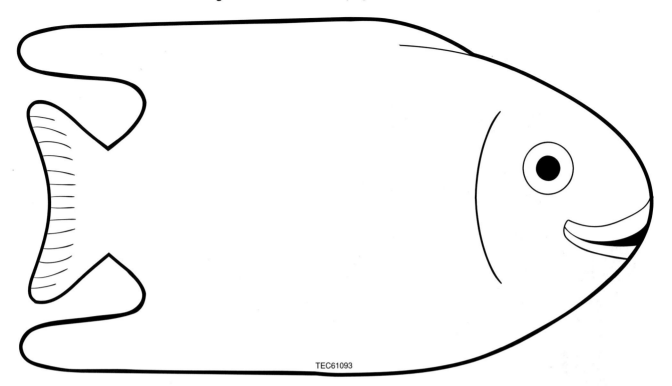

TEC61093

Bone Half Patterns
Use with "No Bones About It, We're a Great Class!" on page 9.

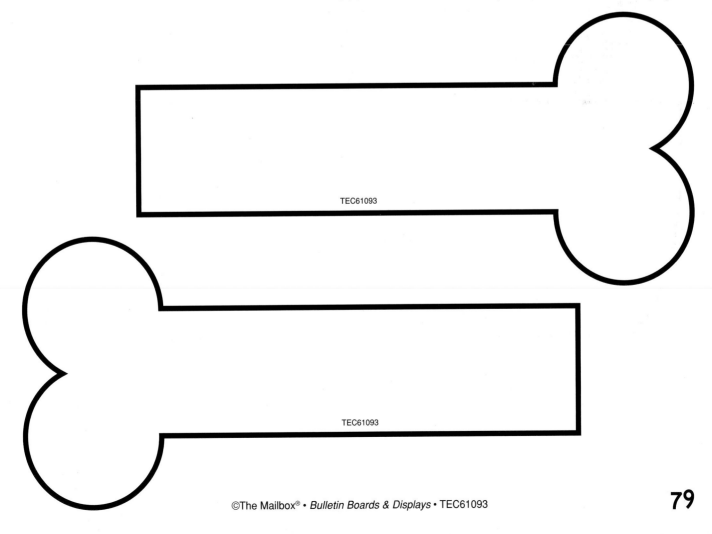

TEC61093

TEC61093

Dog Pattern
Use with "No Bones About It, We're a Great Class!" on page 9 and "Spotlight on Synonyms" on page 55.

TEC61093

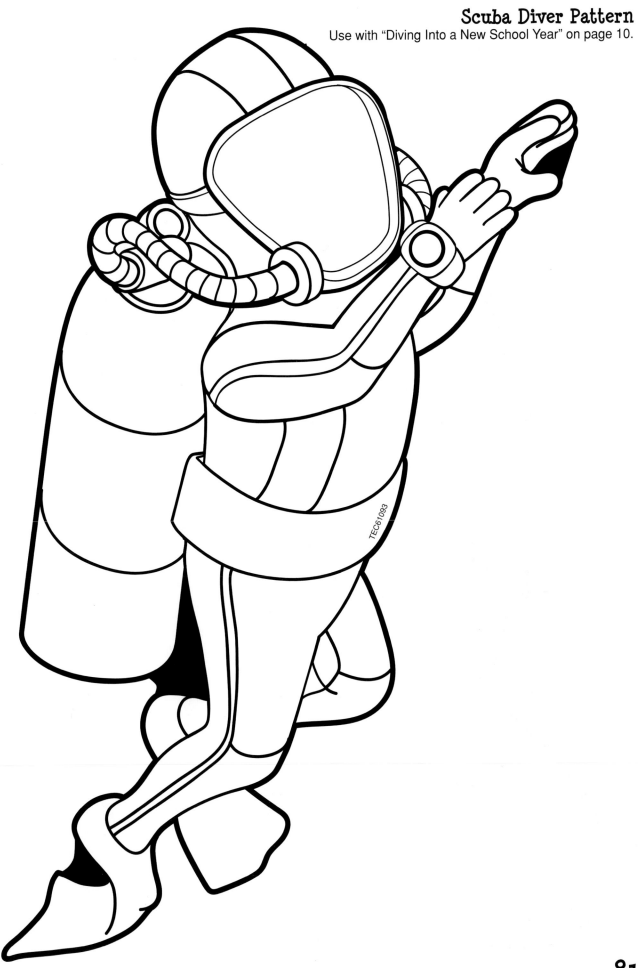

Firecracker Pattern
Use with "Birthdays Are a Blast!" on page 12 and "Dynamite Work!" on page 69.

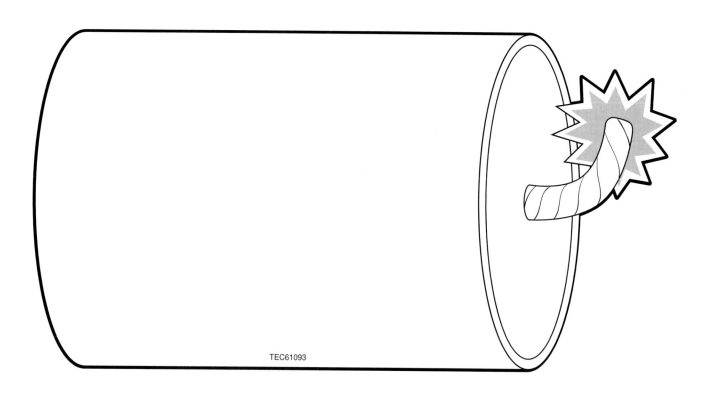

TEC61093

Frog Pattern
Use with "Leaping Together for a Tidy Pad" on page 12.

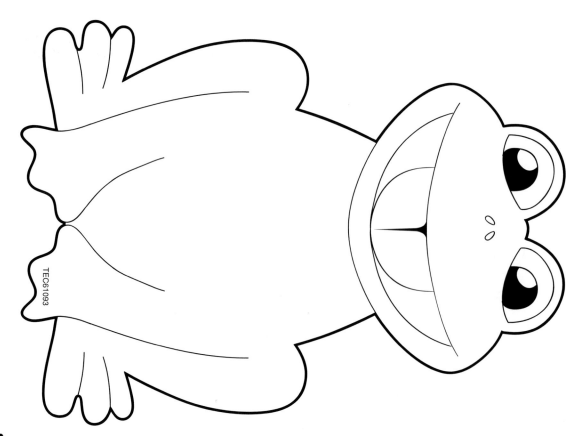

TEC61093

Apple Pattern
Use with "Just 'Ripe' Contractions" on page 13.

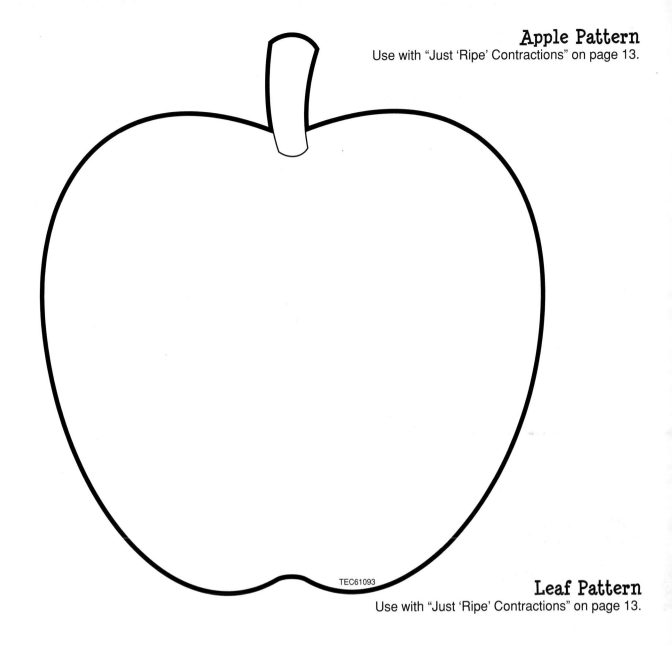

TEC61093

Leaf Pattern
Use with "Just 'Ripe' Contractions" on page 13.

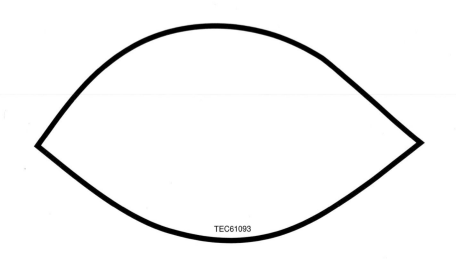

TEC61093

Squirrel Pattern
Use with "We're Nuts About School!" on page 14.

TEC61093

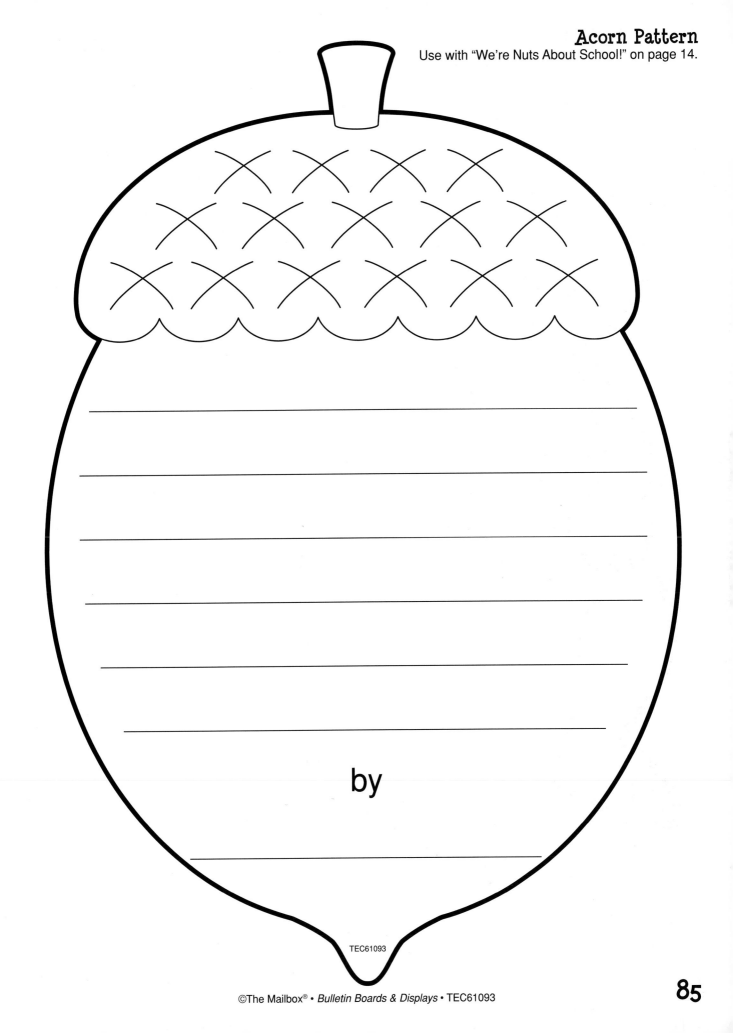

by

TEC61093

Boat Pattern
Use with "A Wave of New Holidays" on page 14.

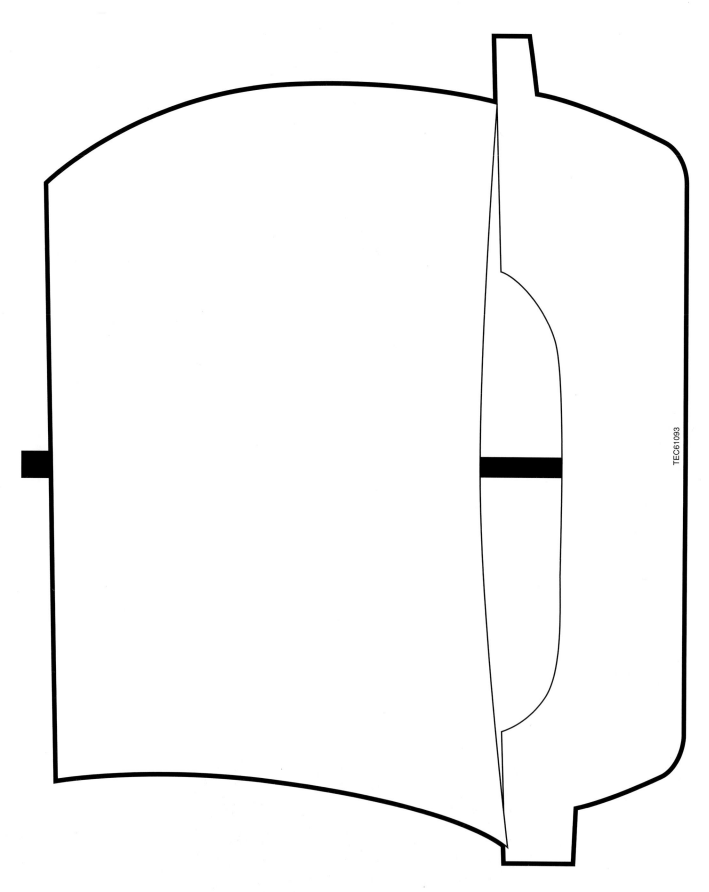

TEC61093

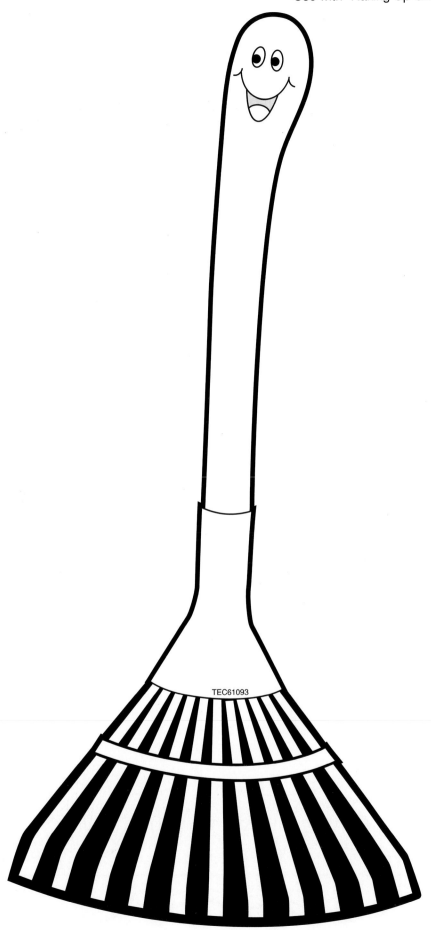

TEC61093

Scarecrow Pattern

Use with "A Harvest of Excellent Work" on page 17.

TEC61093

TEC61093

Pilgrim Pattern
Use with "Plurals Aplenty" on page 20.

TEC61093

Corn Patterns
Use with "Plurals Aplenty" on page 20.

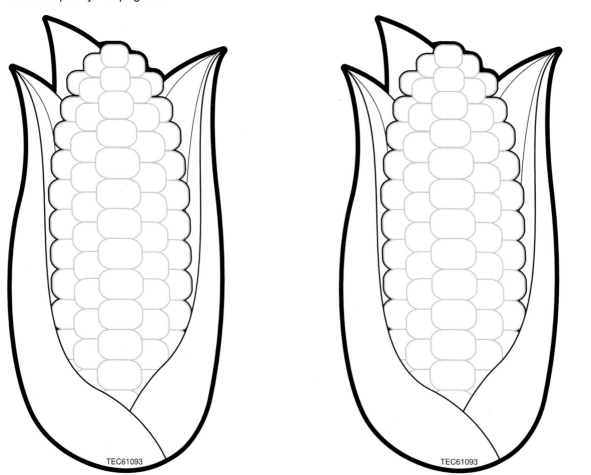

TEC61093

TEC61093

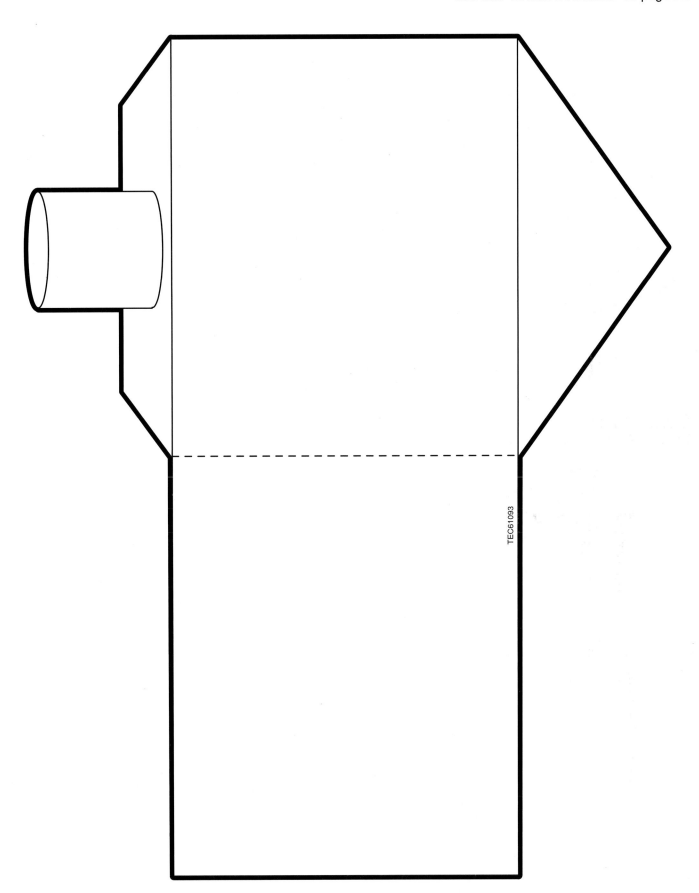

TEC61093

Gift Box Pattern
Use with "Giving Literary Gifts" on page 23.

Book Title and Author:

Setting:

_____

Object:

_____

Word:

_____

Definition: _____

_____

_____

_____

Character:

_____

Description:

_____

_____

_____

TEC61093

TEC61093

Candy Cane Pattern
Use with "Welcome to Our Sweet Classroom!" on page 24.

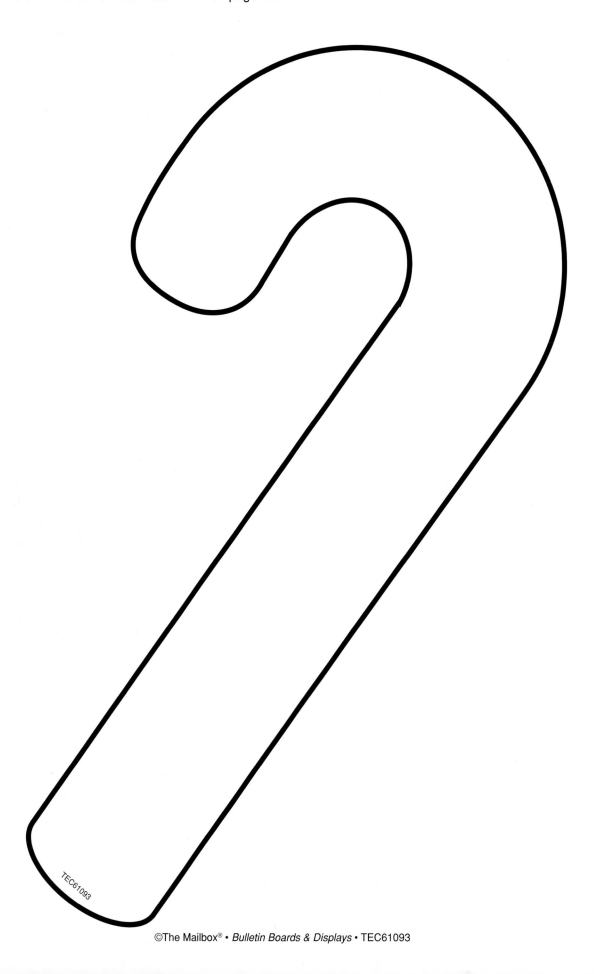

TEC61093

TEC61093

Ice Skate Pattern

Use with "Skating Into Winter Fun" on page 25 and "Skating Into Descriptive Writing" on page 30.

TEC61093

TEC61093

Dove Pattern
Use with "Peaceful Solutions" on page 31.

TEC61093

TEC61093

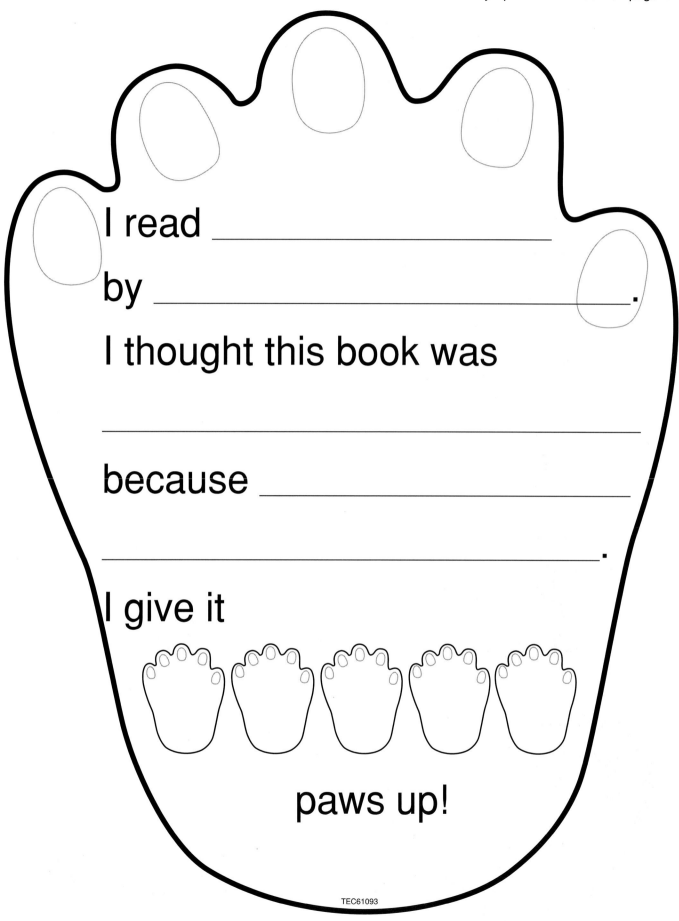

I read _____

by _____.

I thought this book was

_____

because _____

_____.

I give it

paws up!

Snowpal Pattern
Use with "A Blizzard of Blends" on page 29 and "It's Cold Outside!" on page 31.

TEC61093

TEC61093

Heart Character Pattern

Use with "Heartfelt Acts of Kindness" on page 32.

TEC61093

TEC61093

Toad Pattern

Use with "'Toad-ally' Awesome Solid Figures" on page 36.

TEC61093

Bee Pattern

Use with "Buzzing About Adjectives" on page 36, "Bee's Place" on page 66, and "Busy Bees" on page 72.

Basket Pattern
Use with "Look Who's Hatching" on page 37 and "Check Out Our 'Egg-cellent' Work!" on page 40.

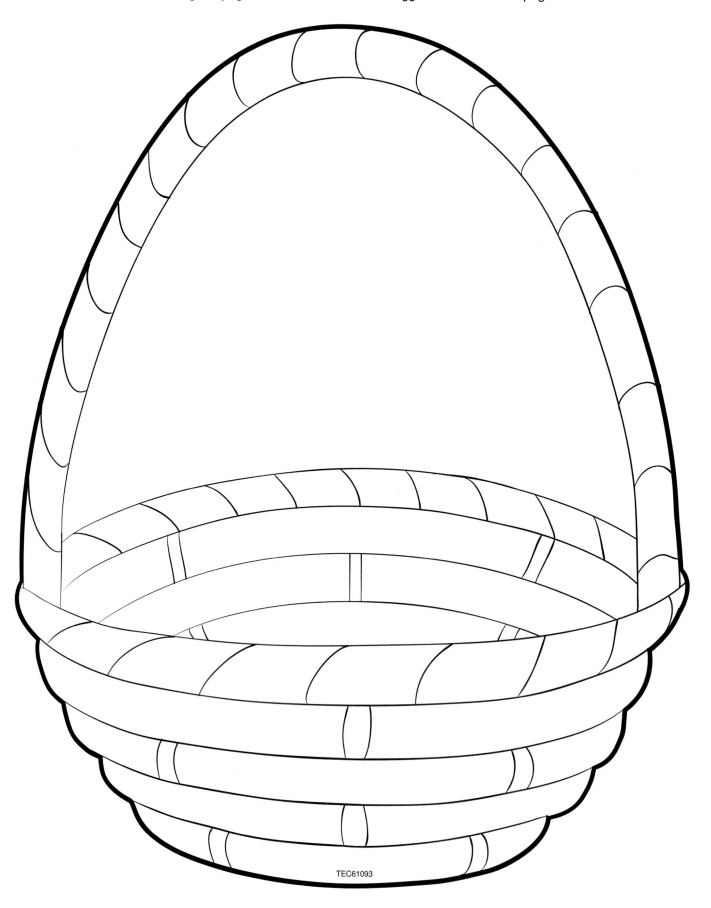

TEC61093

TEC61093

TEC61093

Clutter Bug Pattern
Use with "Don't Be a Clutter Bug" on page 40.

TEC61093

Jelly Bean Pattern
Use with "Jelly Bean Math" on page 41.

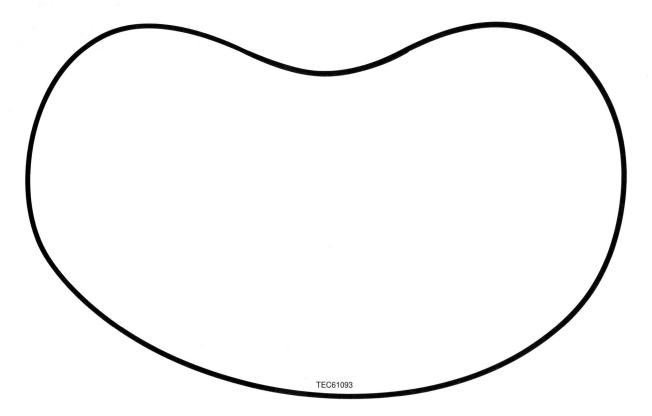

TEC61093

108

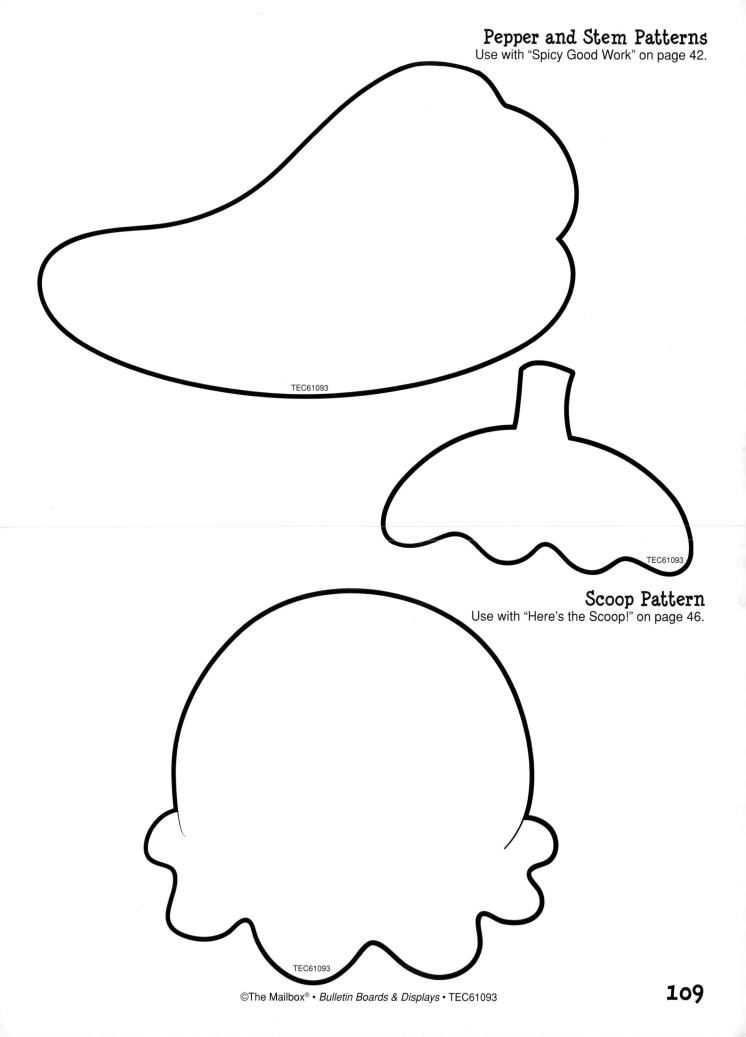

TEC61093

TEC61093

Scoop Pattern
Use with "Here's the Scoop!" on page 46.

TEC61093

Bear and Sombrero Patterns

Use with "Hola, Amigo!" on page 43.

TEC61093

TEC61093

TEC61093

Soccer Player Pattern
Use with "Kick a Goal for Spelling Success!" on page 45.

TEC61093

TEC61093

Sun Pattern
Use with "Sunny Synonyms" on page 47.

TEC61093

TEC61093

Pool Toy Patterns
Use with "Jump Into Parts of Speech" on page 49.

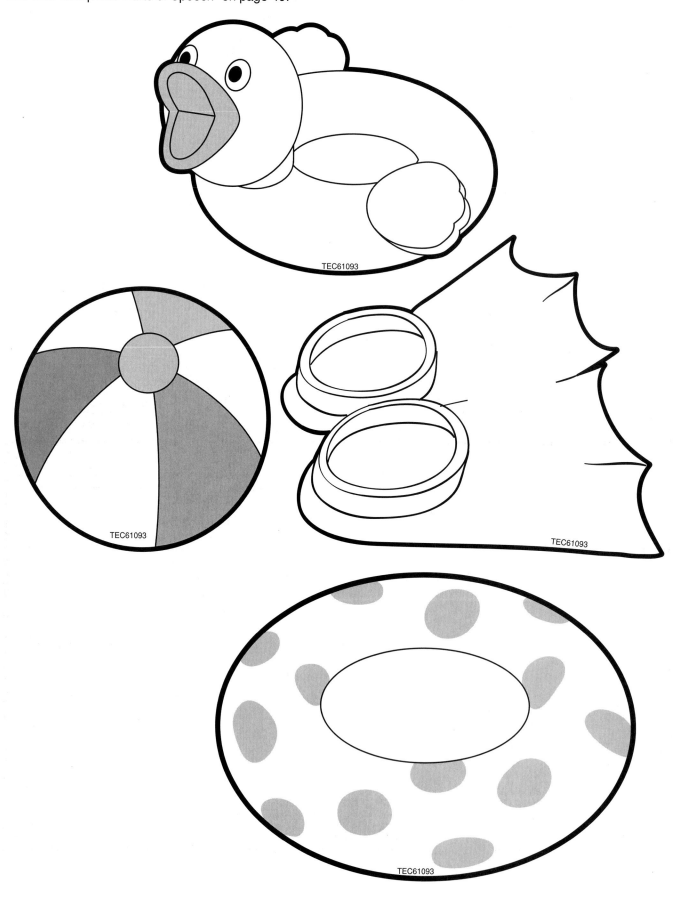

TEC61093

TEC61093

TEC61093

TEC61093

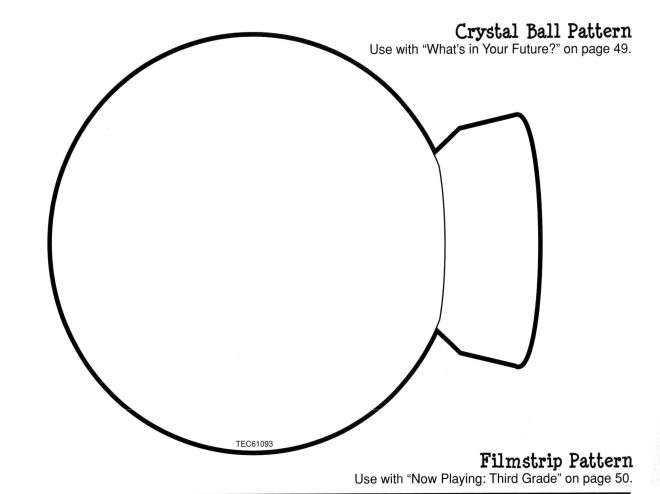

TEC61093

Filmstrip Pattern
Use with "Now Playing: Third Grade" on page 50.

TEC61093

Director's Clapboard Pattern
Use with "Now Playing: Third Grade" on page 50.

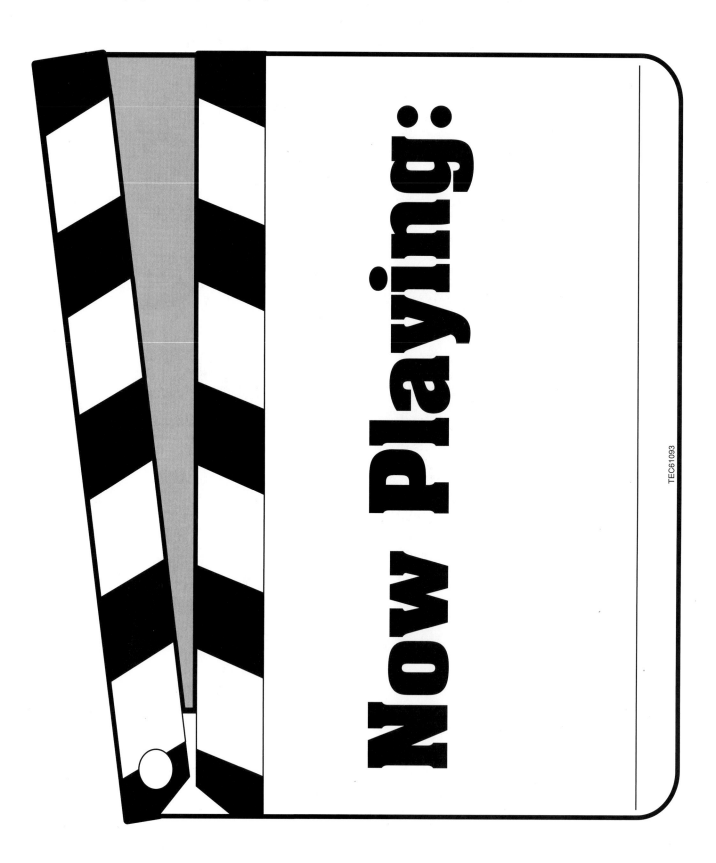

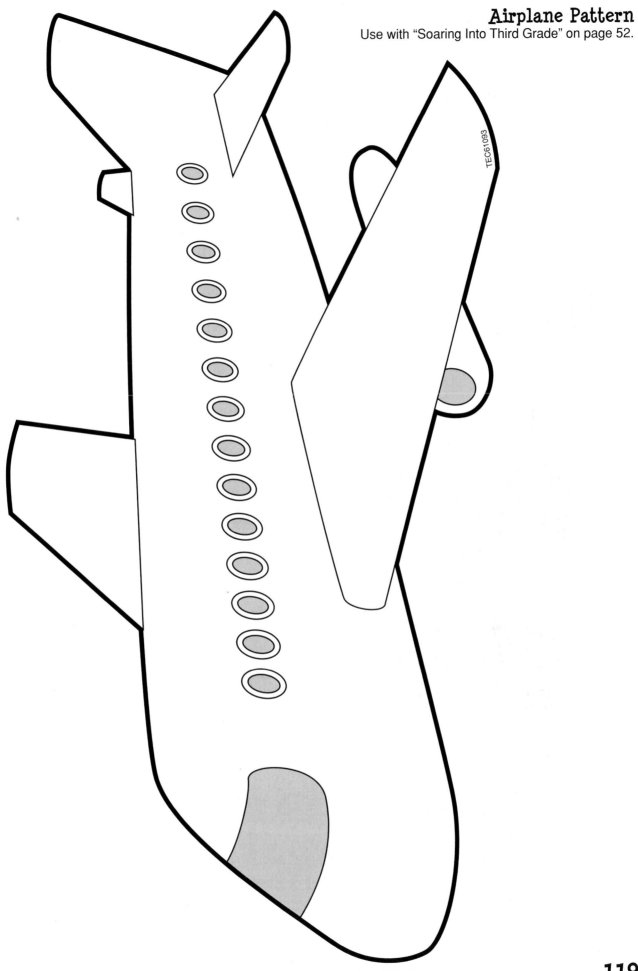

TEC61093

T-Shirt Pattern
Use with "Wash Day the ABC Way" on page 53.

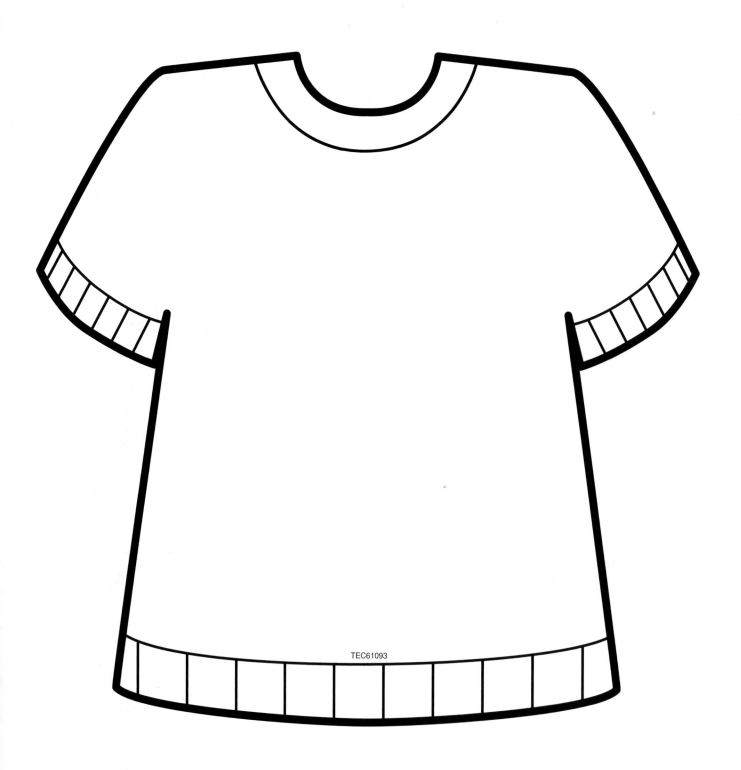

TEC61093

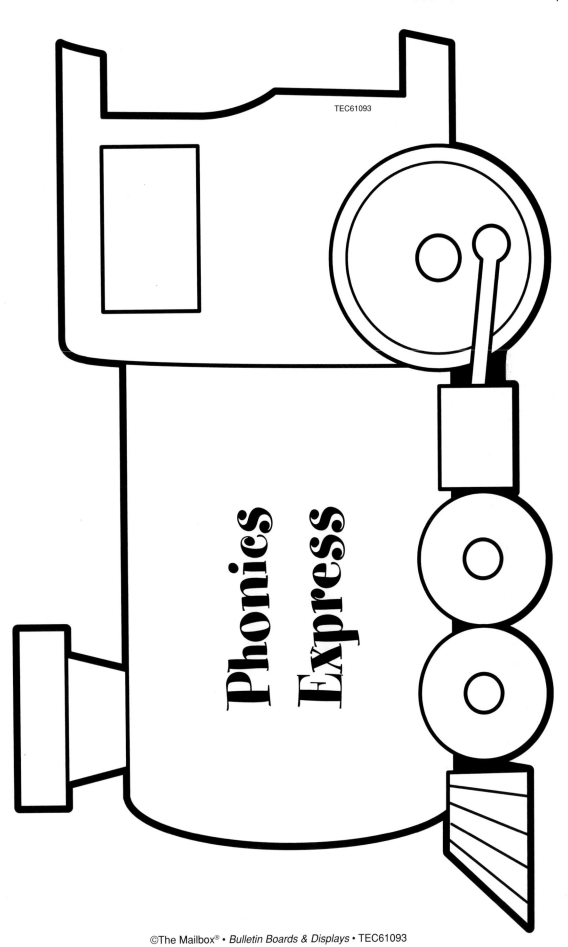

TEC61093

Phonics Express

Banana Pattern
Use with "'A-peel-ing' Adjectives" on page 54.

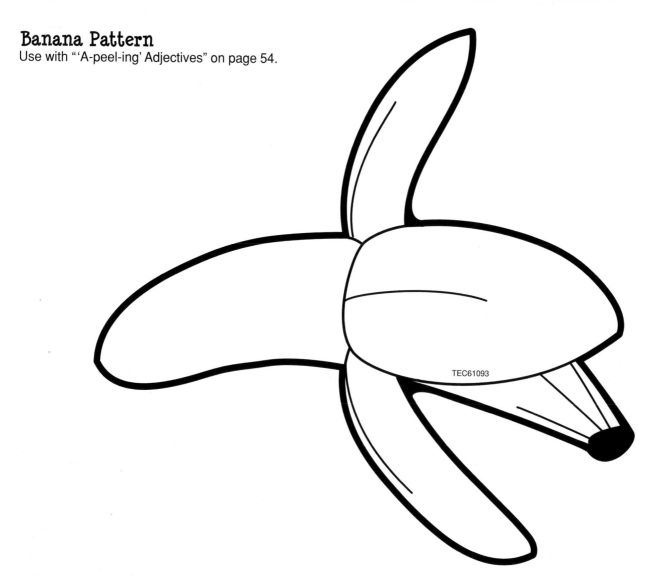

TEC61093

Flashlight Pattern
Use with "Spotlight on Synonyms" on page 55.

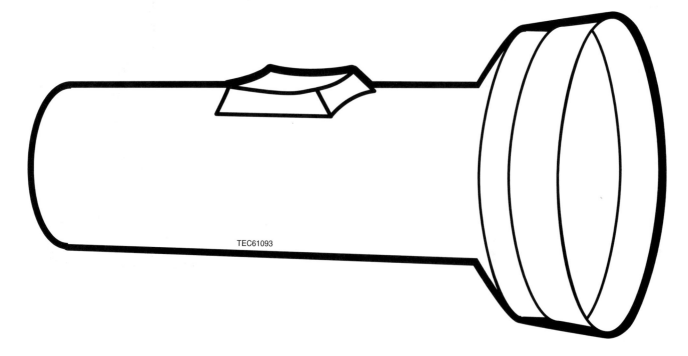

TEC61093

TEC61093

Owl Pattern

Use with "Whoooo's Cool in Your Book?" on page 57 and "How else could the story have ended?" on page 59.

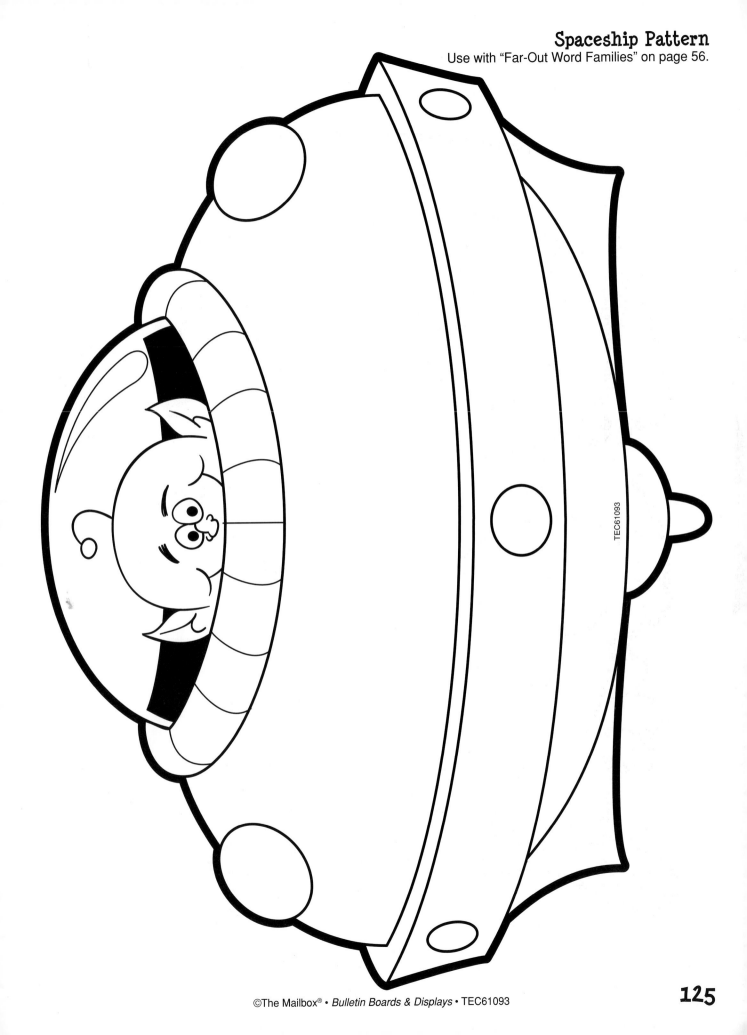

TEC61093

Character Award

Use with "Whoooo's Cool in Your Book?" on page 57.

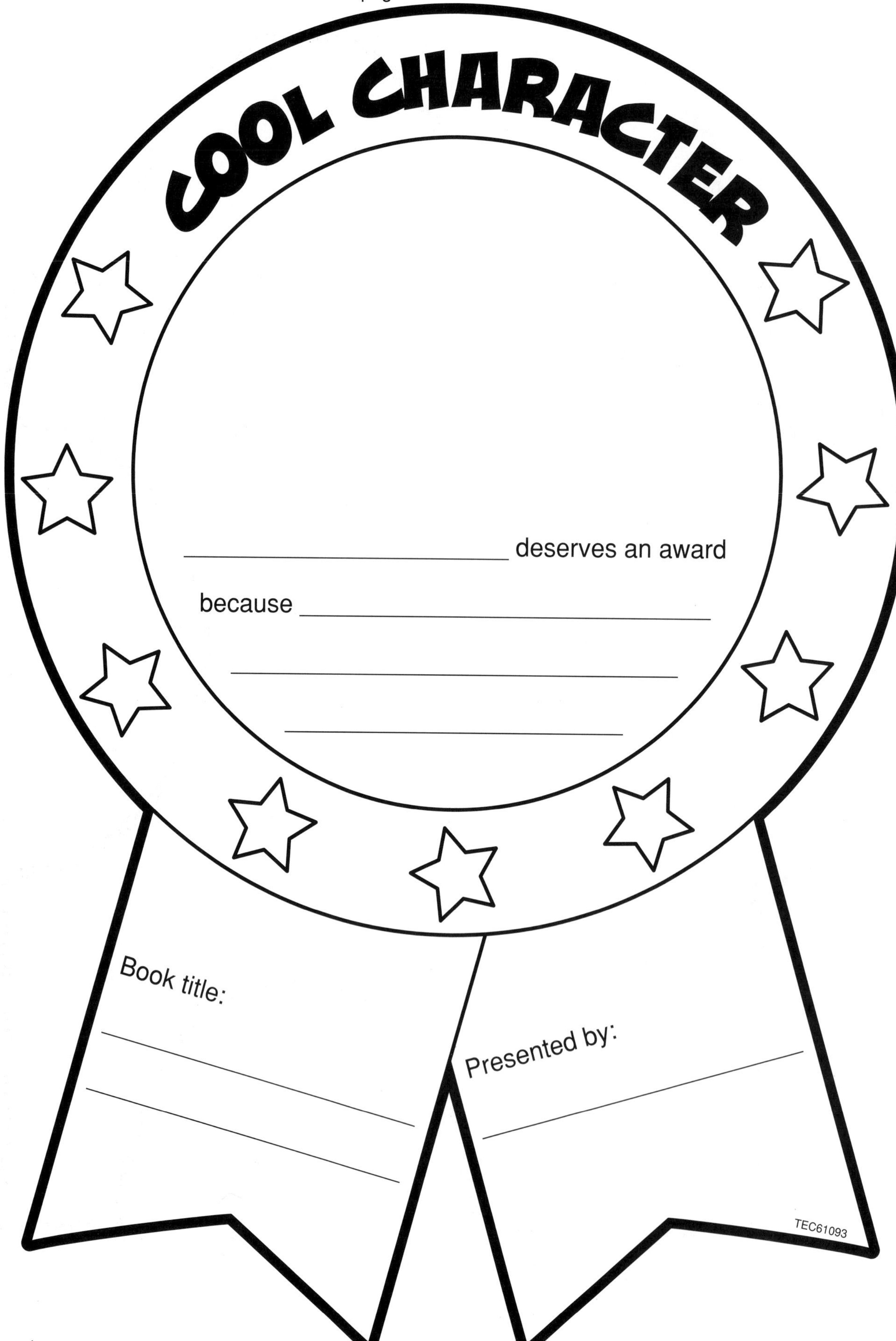

COOL CHARACTER
_______________ deserves an award
because _______________
Book title:
Presented by:
TEC61093

TEC61093

Fishbowl Pattern
Use with "Suffix Swimmers" on page 60.

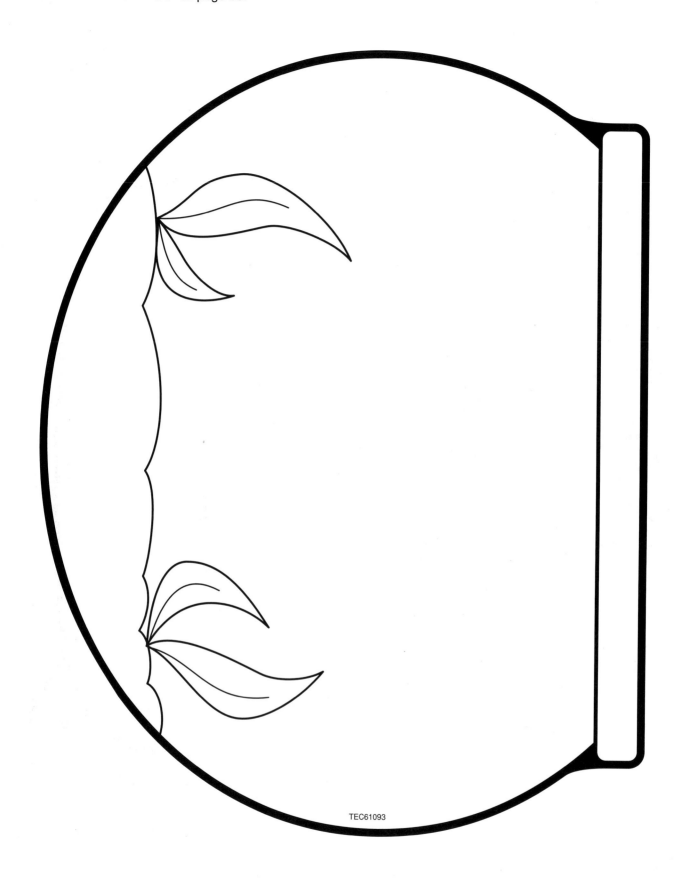

TEC61093

TEC61093

Cookie Jar Pattern
Use with "Cookie Computation" on page 61.

TEC61093

TEC61093

 _____ name **Real-World Math!**	**Sports**	**Coupons**
Menus	**Catalogs**	**Recipes**

Person Patterns
Use with "Rainbow Favorites" on page 62.

TEC61093

TEC61093

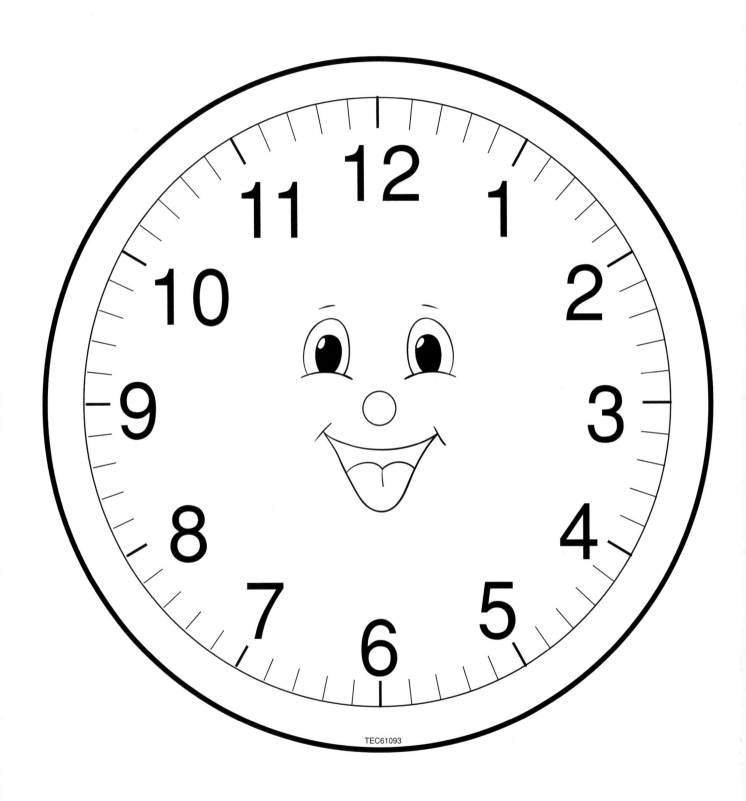

TEC61093

Cheese Patterns

Use with "Mathematical Munchies" on page 65.

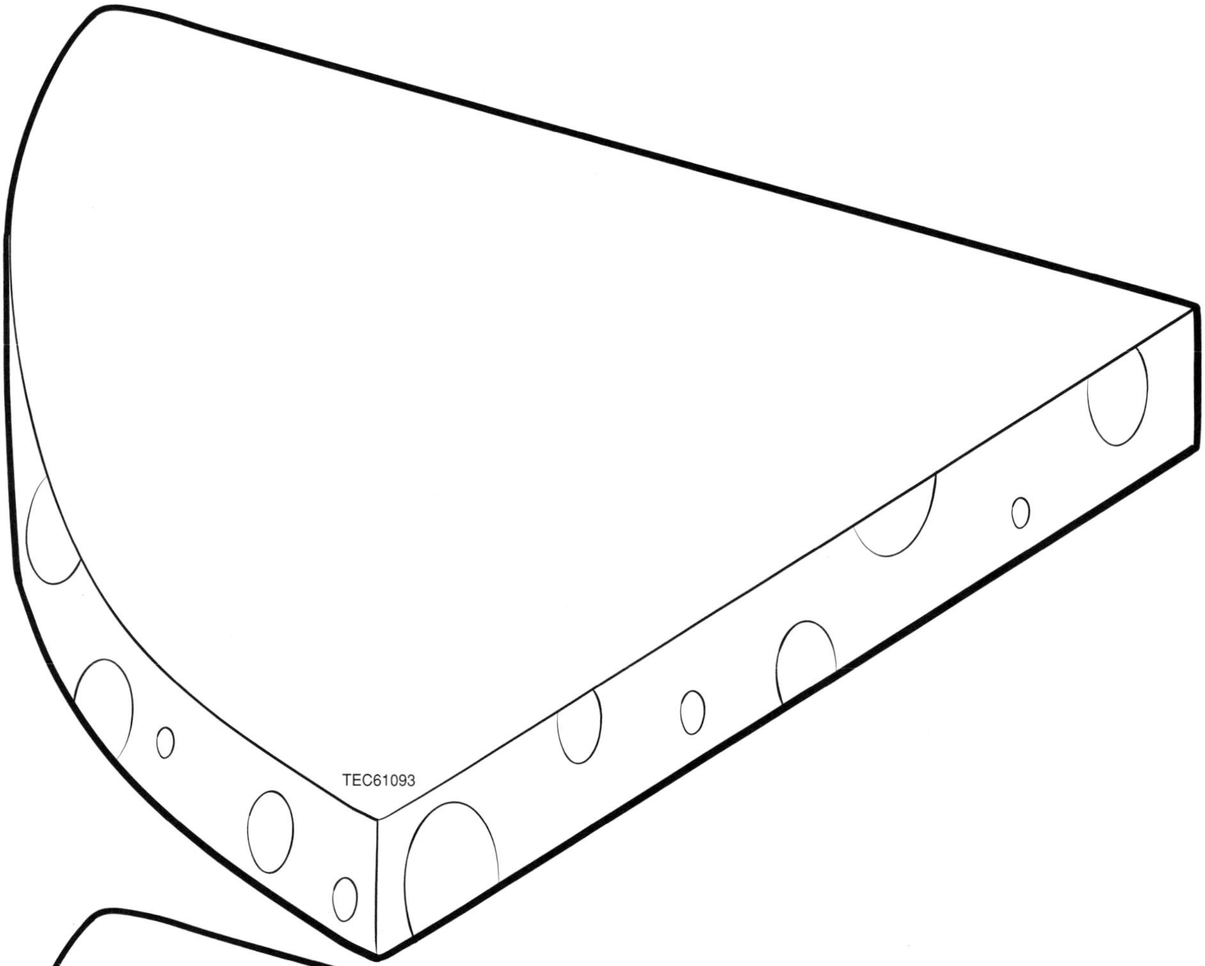

TEC61093

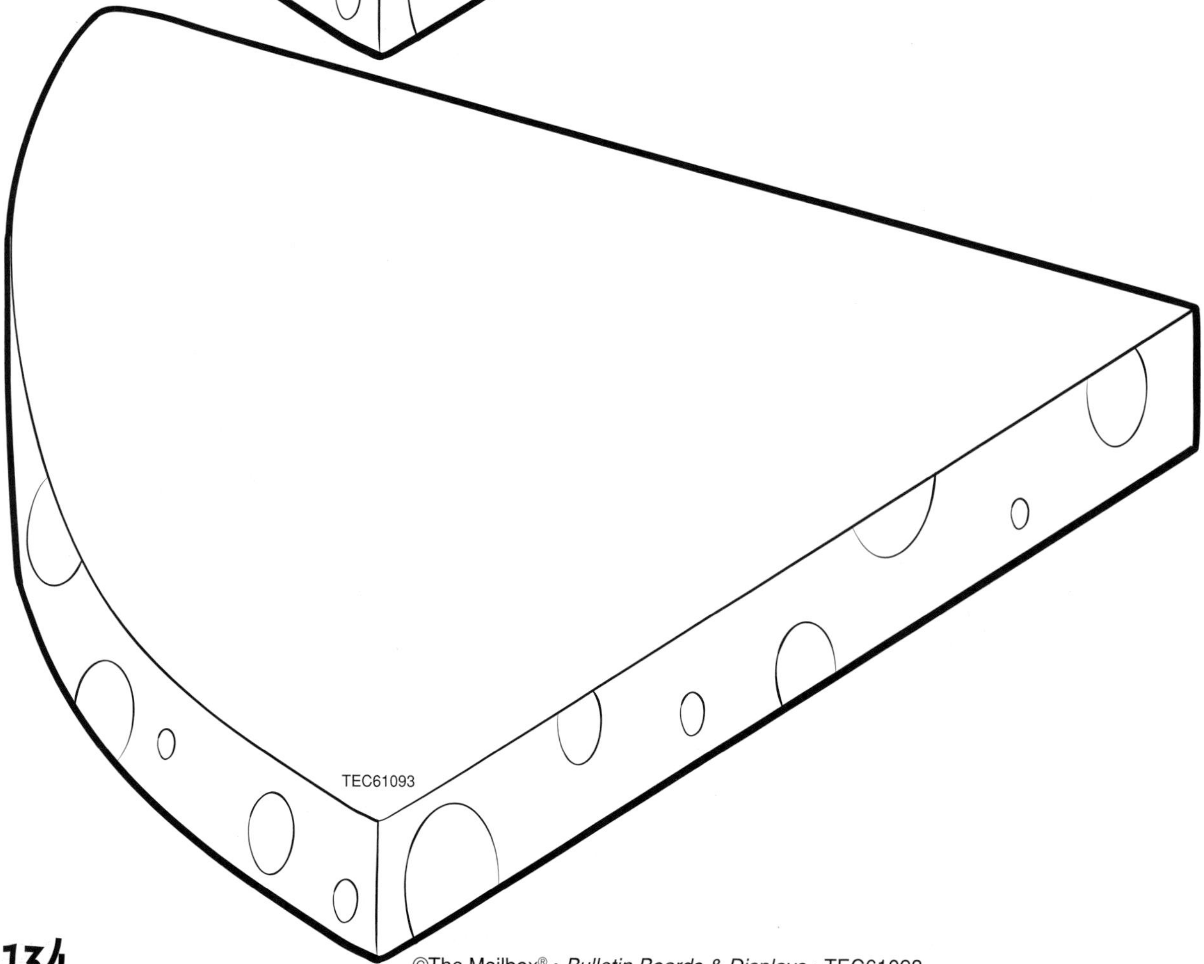

TEC61093

TEC61093

Hot-Air Balloon Pattern

Use with "Flying High With Math!"
on page 65.

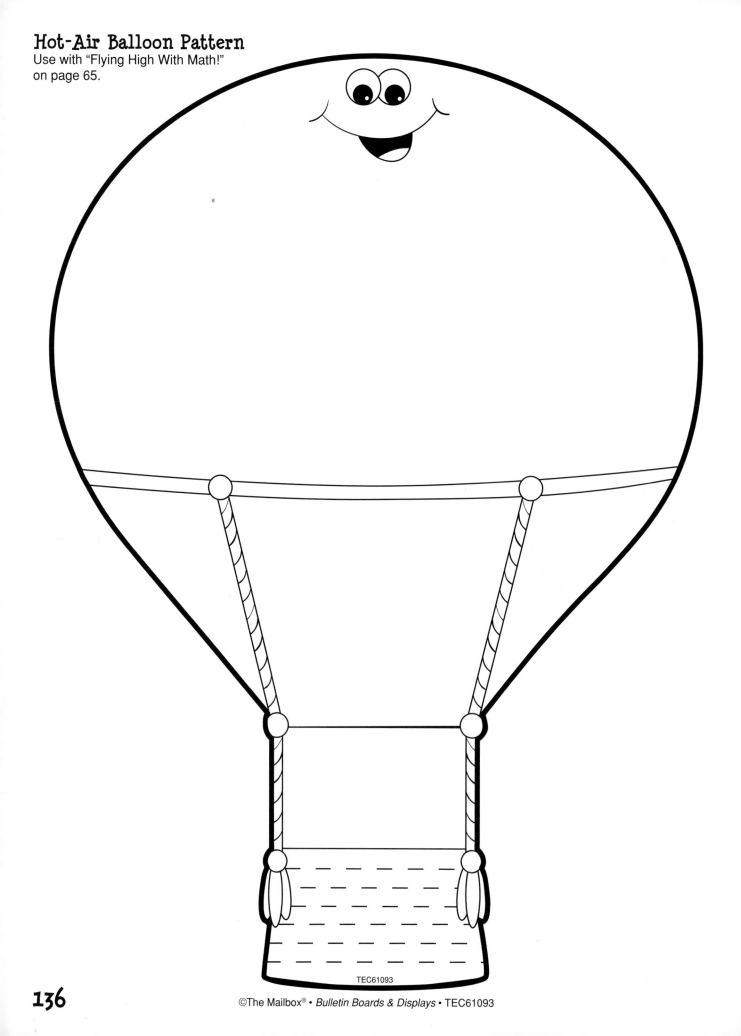

TEC61093

TEC61093

TEC61093

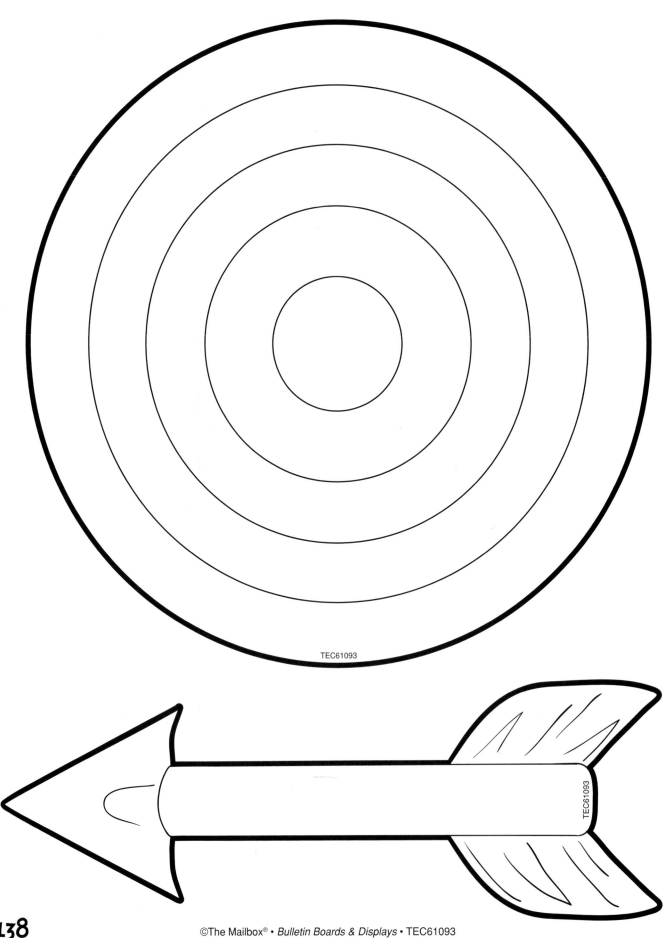

TEC61093

TEC61093

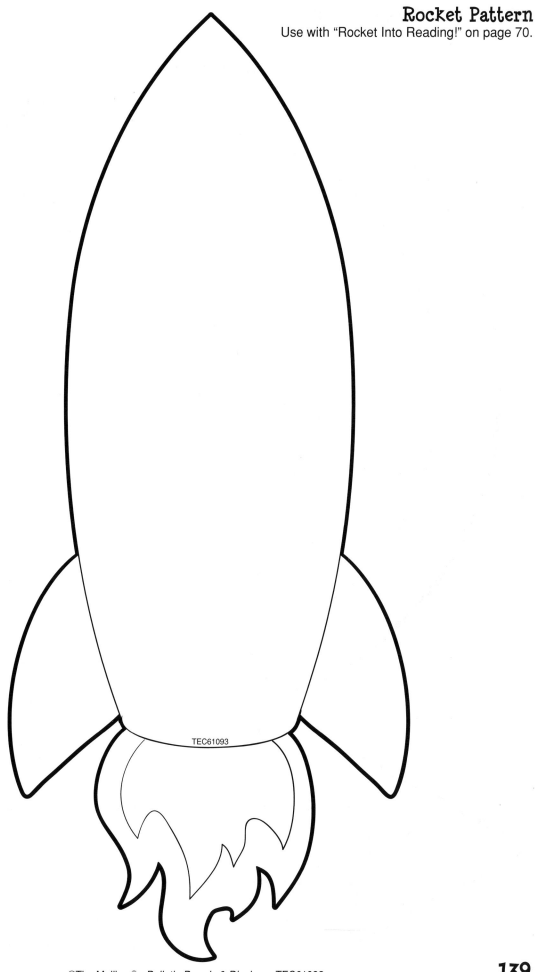

TEC61093

Star Pattern
Use with "Ms. Smith's Shining Stars!" on page 67.

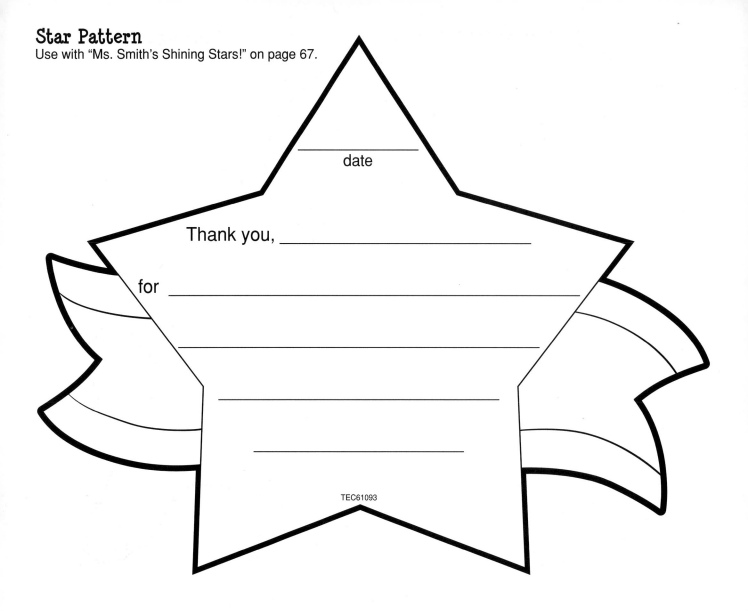

date

Thank you, _____

for _____

_____

_____

_____

TEC61093

Racecar Pattern
Use with "On the Fast Track" on page 67.

TEC61093

140

TEC61093

TEC61093

TEC61093

Index

Pattern Index